ALSO BY LAURA KIPNIS

Against Love:
A Polemic

Bound and Gagged:
Pornography and the Politics of Fantasy in America

Ecstasy Unlimited:
On Sex, Capital, Gender, and Aesthetics

THE FEMALE THING

THE FEMALE THING

DIRT, SEX, ENVY, VULNERABILITY

LAURA KIPNIS

PANTHEON BOOKS, NEW YORK

All rights reserved. Published in the United States by Pantheon
Books, a division of Random House, Inc., New York, and in Canada
by Random House of Canada Limited, Toronto.

Pantheon Books and colophon are registered
trademarks of Random House, Inc.

Library of Congress Cataloging-in-Publication Data
Kipnis, Laura.
The female thing : dirt, sex, envy, vulnerability / Laura Kipnis.
p.   cm.
Includes bibliographical references.
ISBN 0-375-42417-2
1. Women—Psychology.   2. Feminism.   3. Women—Social
conditions.   I. Title.
HQ1206.K475 2006   305.42—dc22   2006043794

www.pantheonbooks.com

Printed in the United States of America
First Edition
2   4   6   8   9   7   5   3   1

CONTENTS

PREFACE

I confess: I have a female thing. Or maybe I have a "thing" about the female thing, or about things female, but as a female, I don't see how you can avoid it—this *thing* that makes women different from men. It's pretty much the defining feature of the female condition.

I'm speaking of the female psyche, of course. Please read what follows as an account of the female psyche at the twenty-first-century mark, which is to say, in the aftermath of second-wave feminism and partway to gender equality, both factors having put many female things into question lately. Or read it as an account of one such female psyche—but you have to start somewhere, right? Where better than a self-inventory: climbing on the couch, shaking out the monkeys. Let me tell you, we're talking about some seriously conflicted inner terrain at the moment, given everything that's happened—or maybe more to the point, failed to happen—in terms of the female thing. I'm talking about gender progress and all the impediments to it, needless to say, since when it comes to the female situation, contradictions speckle the landscape, like ingrown hairs after a bad bikini wax.

Female progress—how's that going? Let's see. Gender barriers have largely crumbled (some exceptions remain), the dominant paradigms of patriarchy have mainly eroded (some exceptions remain), women have increasing economic independence from men if they choose to (though many don't). But then you keep stumbling across the tracks of a certain . . . *ambivalence*. No, not the "backlash" against feminism—I mean the ambivalence among women themselves.

Obviously, social progress is always a stop-start sort of affair. For one thing, the inner lives of the protagonists aren't always on the advance team, so to speak; social change goes whizzing past your ears, with the backwardish psyche—not always quite so amenable to change—bringing up the rear. It's sometimes been said that a colonized mentality far outlasted the political conditions of colonialism; Soviet Communism crumbled virtually overnight, but the inner apparatchik lives on. So too with female progress, it appears.

In other words, feminism came up against an unanticipated opponent: *the inner woman*. If something remains a little obdurate about female inequality after the last forty years or so of activism and protesting, obviously there's no shortage of external culprits to hold accountable: the Media, the Old Boys' Club, the Double Shift. And then we have the culprits closer to home. No, not *men* (though that's pleasantly self-exonerating)—I'm speaking of the collaborator within. Not to point fingers, but without substantial female compliance, wouldn't masculine privilege pretty soon find itself crammed in with all the other debris in the trash can of history? When it comes to male power or female subjection, or whatever you want to call the current arrangement between the sexes, the complicity on the part of women themselves is . . . well, let's just say it's "complicated."

As are women's relations with individual men, consequently, lending a certain bristly, less-than-jolly quality to such interactions in recent years, with the male-female bond (most women are, after all, heterosexual) crashing up against the jagged reefs of gender reform. Of course, it's easy enough to blame all this on men, too, and many of us do, happily locating new male deficiencies on a regular basis. Thus political demands for civic rights and social equality soon gave way to demands for domestic reform—*Make them share the fucking housework*—which soon gave way to calls for a complete overhaul of the male psyche: *Make them talk about their goddamn feelings.* (It turns out they were just waiting to be asked and have yet to shut up.) The small problem is that despite their numerous inadequacies, these men still invariably have something that many women seem to *want*, and want *badly* (their attention, their love, their sperm for all the aspiring moms). Put all this conflicted female craving and ambivalence into the hopper and some pretty fitful sociosexual arrangements emerge. More on this to come.

Feminism has been a universal movement, though the specifics are everywhere different. Still, women across the globe are suspended between progress and tradition in one form or another (or everywhere that modernity has entered the picture, with the rest of the world soon to follow). But the traditional forms persist, soldiering on even in the most "advanced" places, paradoxically—even among the white middle-class and upper-middle-class women who are the main subjects of this book, who are supposed to be the vanguard class when it comes to gender progress, and whose "emancipation" should be setting the benchmark for the global female march toward equality, yet who remain so *fettered* in so many traditionally feminine ways. Foot binding (the conventional emblem of fettered femininity) has all sorts of cosmopolitan equivalents, though the happy new development is that they're now entirely self-imposed. What follows is a catalog of fetters, a chronicle of impasses—including those within feminism itself. Yes, even at the epicenter of Western feminism, the traditional female constraints have an interesting way of reinsinuating themselves, like a scolding grandmother, covering everything with chintz and ruffles, from the couch to social policy recommendations. But when the old feminine types start reappearing in a feminist guise—the female scold, the shrinking violet, the castrating bitch, the sexless mom—it's probably time to clean house.

Among the many "things" that don't yield to progress, foremost would be women's relation to the female body. This should not come as news—look around! Self-loathing abounds, even when it's masked as "self-affirmation." So let's just look it in the face, so to speak. There's a charming saying about women: pull their skirts over their heads, and they all look the same. It falls to me to report that this is indeed true, since if certain aspects of the female condition are mired in tradition, the social consequences of possessing a female anatomy would be central among those things. Having one of these things instead of one of the other things in a culture that still hands out social power and resources on the basis of what kind of anatomy you've been assigned invariably structures the female experience here on earth, and how could this not leave its big pawprint on interior life? Not that female anatomy dictates *what* a woman is or has to be; but it dictates the female condition, and it will do so as long as anatomical differences between the sexes continue to matter. (But no, we're not hardwired like salamanders either, and nothing about gender is mysteriously "encoded" somewhere in the recesses of our genes making men and women what they are; it's a question of the stories we make up to tell each other about the differences between the sexes, stories that are constantly changing and will certainly change some more.) The endless female beautifying and self-improving have yet to mitigate the anatomical situation, though not for lack of trying.

So, let's say that you've set out to map female inner life—for fun, or because it's there, or to see whether Freud was actually right about any of it. You go left, you go right, and what do you keep finding but that very *thing,* imprinted on the very core of the self. What follows is an updated topography of the female psyche, along with notes on the four primary regions I've encountered there: Envy, Sex, Dirt, and Vulnerability. (Perhaps there are others I've missed; please consult your own interiority.) Well, it's a provisional topography, anyway: maps are always being updated—new roads are built, borders shift, suburbs sprawl. Please feel free to append where necessary. A chapter is devoted to each of these regions, exploring the local conflicts and uneven developments and political miscalculations: a series of bulletins on the female predicament (in one corner of the world, at least).

THE FEMALE THING

1

ENVY

Over the course of human history, cultures have endlessly vacil-
lated when it comes to describing the differences between the
sexes. For some reason, there's been a certain fickleness. A male
characteristic in one society is a female characteristic in another;
at one moment men and women are opposites that attract, at
another they're counterparts who repel; they're essentially similar or they're essentially different, though typically not both at
once. Whereas in our time, in the wake of feminism and the
commotion about "roles" and the consequent sexual unrest, it's
now entirely possible for women to be both different *and* similar
to men simultaneously, which promotes a certain confusion
among the gal set, bouncing back and forth like tennis balls between competing theories of what women *naturally are* versus
what women *can become,* or whether women should act more
like men ("strong") or more like powerful women ("strong"), at
least once the remaining impediments to gender equality are
finally overcome (society, bad self-esteem, the wage gap).

In other words, being female at this point in history is an especially conflicted enterprise, like Birkstenstocks with Chanel,
or trying to frown after a Botox injection. But we should be get-

ting used to it, since looking back thirty years or so, you can see the same dichotomies already peeking out from behind contending brands of second-wave feminism. In one corner we had Feminism Plan A: Strive for empowerment, smash those glass ceilings, sport-fuck like the guys, celebrate "strong women"—*"You go, Mrs. Thatcher"*—and impugn the intelligence of the opposite sex with frequency. In the other corner was Feminism Plan B: Demand respect for women's inherent *differences* from men, for our nurturing capacities, our innate moral compass, our emotional intuitiveness, our built-in process-oriented . . . you know . . . process. Women's power inheres in our bodies, our childbearing capabilities, our female sensuality—all of which deeply terrify men and society.

So which one should it be? The Feisty Feminist or the Eternal Feminine, careers or motherhood, ballsy or baby-doll—or why not all at once! But the truly fascinating question is how it came about that whichever one you chose, what was once construed as a *liberation* movement somehow ended up producing more dichotomies and more impasses and the perennial sense that despite everything that's been gained, something's invariably *missing*. Of course, in hindsight we see that under Plan A, women demanded to have what men have, without stopping to consider whether it was worth having, or whether men really even possessed it in the first place—and that "empowerment" was always a word with a certain overcompensatory ring to it. And that under Plan B, the essential-womanhood thing quickly started looking like an updated version of traditional femininity,

especially once the whole goddess-worshipping New Age ve-
neer got scratched off.

So where does that leave gender progress?

Let's recall that a long time before either Plan A or Plan B
came down the pike, femininity was already an "empowerment
program" for women. Appearances to the contrary, femininity
was never about being some kind of delicate flower; it was tacti-
cal: a way of securing resources and positioning women as ad-
vantageously as possible on an uneven playing field, given the
historical inequalities and anatomical disparities that make up
the wonderful female condition. Femininity was the method for
creatively transforming female disadvantages into advantages,
basically by doing what it took to form strategic alliances with
men: enhancing women's appeal and sexual attractiveness with
time-honored stratagems like ritual displays of female incompe-
tence aimed at subtly propping up men's (occasionally less than
secure) sense of masculine prowess. Thus, lacking body mass,
women made a virtue out of delicacy (often a rather steely delicacy); stuck with not just bearing but also raising the children,
women promoted the sanctity of motherhood; deprived of
upper-body strength, women made men carry things; afflicted
by capricious hormonal fluctuations, women used crying as
a form of interpersonal leverage; restricted from the public
sphere, women commandeered domestic life; shut out of de-
cent employment, gals adopted a "pay-to-play" strategy—men
had to pay for sex, with dinners, rings, and homes. Men are also
required to kill spiders. All this took some considerable effort:

achieving what looks like a passive aim often requires large amounts of activity, as someone once said. (Okay, it was Freud.) The point is that femininity assumes that the world isn't going to change and endeavors to secure advantages for women on that basis.*

Then came feminism. Feminists saw the unequal playing field differently: they wanted to level it. Feminism assumes that things *can* change—even men—and bets the bankroll on gender progress. There's no doubt that feminism has claimed a lot of social terrain over the last three or four decades, has made numerous inroads into the female psyche and overhauled gender identities across the population, even among those who don't talk the talk. Face it, we *all* inhabit a postfeminist world: it was, after all, feminism that brought women equal treatment under the law, voting rights, access to public life, some progress toward pay equity, and so on, and even among the most diehard "I like being a woman" set, you don't find too many arguing with the right to own property or wanting to hand back the vote or anything silly like that.

If the female condition seems especially perplexing at the moment, the reason, it becomes evident, is that women are left straddling two rather incompatible positions. Feminism ("Don't call me honey, dickhead") and femininity ("I just found the

---

*It has sometimes been argued that the conditions of femininity have been imposed by patriarchy. Feel free to tell the story this way around, if you prefer—that is, if you don't mind reducing women to the status of passive receptacles as opposed to agents.

world's best push-up bra!") are in a big catfight, nowhere more than within each individual female psyche. The femininity adherents aren't giving up their social rights, while even most diehard feminists aren't about to surrender the advantages that can be secured through deploying femininity when possible— not these days, especially not those of a heterosexual bent. (Honk if you're pro-choice on cosmetics.)

The main reason that feminism and femininity are incompatible is that femininity has a nasty little secret, which is this: femininity, at least in its current incarnation, hinges on sustaining an underlying sense of female inadequacy. Feminism, on the other hand, wants to eliminate female inadequacy, to trounce it as a patriarchal myth, then kick it out of the female psyche for good. The two continue to battle it out, nowhere more than within women's relations to their bodies, which is to say, within the entirety of the female self-relation.

Let's begin with a case study. Our subject is feminist heroine Eve Ensler, the author-impresario behind the worldwide theatrical phenomenon *The Vagina Monologues*. This was followed by *The Good Body*, a one-woman show centering on Ensler's tormented relationship with her slightly protruding post-forties abdomen. According to Ensler, after having said the word "vagina" in public close to a million times, having thought she'd come to terms with possessing a vagina herself, she finally realized that the self-hatred had merely migrated upward to her stomach. Between the obsessive dieting, the exercise, and the agonizing, given all the emotional energy funneled into her stomach over the

years, Ensler laments, that pot belly has been her most significant relationship. Note that even a self-proclaimed radical feminist can't seem to simply jettison the stratagems of femininity
or the norms of beauty culture, despite being armed to the
teeth with feminist theory and analysis. Early in the evening, the
audience is treated to the self-loathing-feminist equivalent of
a money shot, with Ensler yanking blouse up and waistband
down, and yes, there in all its naked shame, perched upon a per-
fectly acceptable body, is indeed a small pot. Ensler works herself into intellectual knots trying to come to terms with these
painful body insecurities, but there's a simple explanation for
the dilemma she can't quite decipher, which is that feminism
and femininity just aren't reconcilable. Though if only internal
gymnastics burned calories, we could *all* have flatter stomachs,
with far fewer hours at the fucking gym.

In other words, the drawback to femininity, as currently construed, is that it can never be successfully attained. Or not once
consumer culture got into the act, since in this configuration,
femininity revolves around the anxiety of female *defectiveness* to
perpetuate itself. Between the truckloads of instruction, the
endless guidance, the chirpy "helpful hints," perpetuating insuf-
ficiency is clearly the objective. In fact, a better name for contemporary femininity would be *the feminine-industrial complex,*
a vast psychocommercial conglomerate financed by women
themselves (though any sex can profiteer) and devoted to churn-
ing out fantastic solutions to the alarming array of psychological problems you didn't know you had ("Are You a Love Addict?";

"Do You Have Night Eating Syndrome?"); social hazards you hadn't even considered (dangerous infections from unsanitized pedicure bowls, the sociopath who could be living next door); and bodily imperfections previously overlooked ("poor pore management," unkempt pubic hair). Why, it's almost as if the whole female condition hinged on some kind of ontological *flaw*. If you're a modern female, unfortunately something's always *broken*. Girls: be thinner, sexier, more self-confident; stop dating creeps; get rid of those yucky zits; and put the pizzazz back in your relationship. Something needs *improving*: your lingerie, your stress levels, your orgasms (or lack of them). Are you in a "toxic friendship"? Is your career in the doldrums? Is your boyfriend lying to you? Why not go organic—eco-chic is hot! Here Are Nine Ways to Reinvent Your Body, Mind, and Social Life—you can do it, all in your spare time, because you're fabulous. Or can be soon—just stop doubting yourself! (Self-doubt is *not* attractive.) Take this quiz, buy this amazing new moisturizing deodorant (underarms get dry, too!), wax your eyebrows: you'll feel *a lot better* once you do.

Eager to feel even minimally less agonized about themselves, the subjects in question enlist in ongoing and usually rather pricey laboring, improving, and self-despair in service to the elusive feminine ideal. But somehow whatever you do, you've failed in advance: there's always that straggly inch-long chin hair, or the cottage-cheese thighs, or just the inexorable march of time to eradicate all previous efforts (even the dewiest ingenue is a Norma Desmond waiting to happen—but keep slathering on that incredibly expensive breakthrough-formula antioxidant moisturizer anyway), and thus the whole endeavor must start up again. Clearly there's nothing exactly "natural" about femininity, given the potions, regimens, and routine discomfort required to achieve it. At its best—which is to say, its most artificial—femininity does have a certain playful frivolity to it: it's fun, it's superficial, it solves the problem of too much spare cash creating an unsightly bulge in your pocketbook. The downside is that women have to fail at femininity precisely to keep working at it, because needless to say, your self-loathing and neurosis are someone else's target quarterly profits.

Yet let's consider the great leap forward for women in the self-improvement sphere. Once much of the oppressive advice was handed down to women by remote authorities: doctors, psychologists, domestic scientists—more often than not male. These days, most of the oppressive advice comes from other women: let's call them Professional Girlfriends—always selflessly ready to aid and comfort another member of the sorority. The top-down management of women's lives (and everything else) by men was called "patriarchy" by second-wave feminists, and blamed for the various ills besetting the female condition. With feminism's declining drawing power, the present condition of women has often been designated "postfeminism." The main difference is this: in place of yesterday's tyrannical husbands and social restrictions, today we have the *girlfriend industry,* and voluntary servitude to self-improvement. Sign up here, because there's a happier, more perfect *you* hidden in there, just waiting to be set free. Be who you truly *are.* Once you've had a makeover, that is. The genius of the girlfriend industries is temporarily alleviating the sense of anxiety and inadequacy they're also so adept at producing, while obscuring the fact that women end up more corseted and restricted than ever.

Recall that Freud's slightly contentious phrase for this bedrock female sense of inadequacy was "penis envy"—which just sounds so retro these days. Who wants some fleshy old appendage swinging between her legs? *Not us,* we're quite happy with our own equipment, thank you! Funnily enough, it's not actually psychiatrists who peddle this idea anymore; it's women themselves, since isn't the notion that "something's missing" the dynamic driving the entirety of women's culture? Pick up the current issue of any women's magazine, tune into a daytime talk show, peruse one of the millions of how-to-land-a-man or how-to-fix-something-about-yourself books, and contemplate the sheer magnitude of *anxiety about the lack of something* on display. If something's missing (relax, not a *penis,* don't be so literal— just *something*), luckily that elusive missing "something" can be creatively marketed under an infinite variety of labels, none of which ever precisely fixes anything, which is why women make the world's most dedicated *consumers,* leaping at the next instant solution to the nonexistent or craftily exacerbated problem, wallets agape. (Purses and pussies: a long-standing symbolic association, by the way.) The female psyche and consumer culture: the world's ultimate codependent couple.

Of course, husbands and babies have been the traditional— and not entirely unsuccessful—mechanisms for assuaging any nagging sense of female incompletion, except that in our time, or let's say from sometime around 1960 on, unfortunately the solution became the problem. Something was *still* missing; husbands and babies *weren't* the answer: you could hear the howls of female dissatisfaction bouncing off the kitchen and nursery walls. Betty Friedan's 1963 book *The Feminine Mystique* had its inception in a questionnaire Friedan sent to her 1947 Smith College classmates, asking if they were happy with their suburban housewife lives; it turned out they were not. Women wanted *more* (educated women especially)—traditionally male prerogatives like careers, for instance. Not coincidentally, all this happened right around when the Pill came on the market: once the technology was finally available to sever sex from reproduction, female dissatisfaction with the maternal role really started escalating; birthrates plummeted. Enter the women's movement, which, come the 1970s (in partnership with recession and the new information economy), began drawing women into the labor force in record numbers. Fast-forward thirty years or so to the new millennium. Now women *have* those careers, and these days the howls of dissatisfaction are bouncing off corporate suites and boardroom walls. Career women want *more*—traditionally female prerogatives like husbands and babies, for instance. Or just . . . something. That ever-missing "something."

On a more positive note: for the first time in history, women *are* relatively free from certain traditional fetters. No longer is womanhood synonymous with motherhood for those who don't so choose: let's hear it for modern birth control! But freedom can be a heavy burden for a girl (well, for the species at large), or so it appears, since a zillion new bodily constraints have instantly blossomed to take the place of the old bodily constraints. One way or another, women just seem to end up defined by their bodies, or defining themselves by their bodies: a source of self-worth, a site of craziness, most likely both. For every bodily advance wrested from nature or society or men, another form of submission magically appears to take its place; for every inch of progress, a newfangled subjugation. And now, most of them self-inflicted! Take the current mania for thinness, the quest for fitness, the war on cellulite. Freed from compulsory childbearing, women have chained themselves to the gym. Once women suffered under whalebone corsets; now your skeleton must show through the skin for that fashionable look. Or consider the popularity of secondary-sex-organ mutilation in those areas of the world where primary-sex-organ mutilation is not the norm—in other words, breast implants. In lieu of foot binding, Manolo Blahniks—surgery optional to reshape recalcitrant feet for a better fit. More irony: here are so-called modern women slicing and dicing body parts to achieve a feminine ideal—and even if "freely chosen," the cut of the knife is just as sharp as back in the village. You hear a lot of talk about "assertiveness" in women's culture today, except you hear it from women shopping for baby-doll outfits, or getting Brazilian bikini waxes, or double-D cup breast implants. "I *like* feeling like a woman," she'll assert (or demur). If there's a "backlash" against feminism, most of those carrying it out these days are women, just trying to "*feel* like women."

But back to the positive: with more control over maternity, record numbers of women are now participating in the workforce, meaning that no longer is womanhood synonymous with economic dependency. Let's hear it for paychecks! In fact, women can now be entirely free from men, should they so choose. Interestingly, it turns out that despite the new possibilities for economic liberty, the majority of women do not so choose. In fact, it turns out there are rather obdurate female longings in regard to dependency on men, despite certain confident pronouncements to the contrary back in those early heady years of the second wave, catchy slogans about vibrators being a girl's best friend and women needing men like fish need bicycles. What do you know: it turns out that fish are devoted cyclists. In fact, the problem these days is that the bicycles seem to be fleeing the fish, or at least fleeing the padlocks and hatcheries. Now women are dedicated to reeling them back, resorting to complicated algorithms about not accepting Saturday night dates later than Tuesday, or staying on the phone longer than the square root of the number of days since the last phone call. What's evident about male-female arrangements at present is this: female dissatisfaction with men is a growth industry, and longing to possess a man doesn't have to include either trusting or particularly liking him.

A tale of two dinner parties. Not typical, not atypical; no big earthshaking events took place—just a couple of cross sections from the sexual zeitgeist.

At the first party, mostly couples, the hostess spent the

evening addressing her husband in tones of such well-honed contempt that Edward Albee could have written the dialogue. In fact, among *all* the married female guests, scorn for husbands was as thick as a wedding album: they had hubbies' number and weren't going to let anyone else at the table miss it. The hostess had a wonderfully subtle way of interrupting her husband—who did indeed have much to say—every time he got to the crucial point in an anecdote, invariably to inform him, in candied tones, of some essential task that needed performing at exactly that moment. *Which you'd notice if you weren't such an insufferable long-winded narcissist.*

"Richard, do you want to pour the coffee or slice the cake?" she interrupted him once again following dinner. *Shut up and help, you self-absorbed egomaniac.* Barely glancing at her, he shot back, "Both," with a triumphant little smirk—*got you, you control freak*—and kept on with what he was saying. *I can't be bothered to care what you think because I've heard it a million times.* In one exchange, two concise lines, was everything there is to say about enmity between the sexes at this moment in history. When Richard failed to slice the cake with enough alacrity, not yet finished with whatever shaggy-dog story he now was on, one of the other wives seated at his end of the table grabbed the knife from him, announcing with a display of eye rolling to the guests, "I'd better do this or we'll be here forever," soliciting the rest of the females present to bond over this bit of typical male buffoonery. All happily did. *Men! Too self-involved to cut a cake! The female struggle continues, one slice at a time!*

A week later, at a second party, an attractive, successful single professional female in her mid- to late thirties with a few glasses of wine under her belt was pronouncing (too loudly for the size of the room) that she wished men *would* treat her more like a sex object, that it's so *boring* to be respected, but men these days are babies—they're all completely threatened by women and afraid of sex, and if you're not twenty, they're not interested because you've got their number. Thus she was forced to date younger men, who hadn't yet retreated from sex (usually her assistants, though this rarely worked out well in the long run), but at least they still know how to *flirt*. It was all very modern and independent, and you could tell just by looking that she was One Strong Babe, except there was a certain note of falseness in the air, between the insistent feistiness and the thinly concealed distress at not having gotten what she disavowed wanting, which was, needless to say, the most traditional thing in the world for a heterosexual female to want despite the post-traditional packaging: a man's love. Which you also suspected might prove impossible to accede to, since this thwarted quest narrative of displeasing candidates and failed tests would hardly allow for the possibility. You started to get the idea that the true attachment was to the story of her disappointment.

Clearly both male presence *and* male absence are equally capable of causing chagrin, each in its own unique way. If women are suspended between wanting to *have* a man and wanting what men *don't have to give,* this nevertheless dissuades few heterosexual women from an abiding commitment to the premise that these men *could* gratify female needs and desires if only they were somehow *different* than they are. Less like men, for one thing.

If only men could be different—more like women, for instance. In the mid-1980s, psychoanalyst Elizabeth Lloyd Mayer started noticing that her female patients' complaints about men seemed to revolve around a certain recurring theme: a fixation on the idea that men are *lacking* something, something crucial. Men are emotionally closed, they're not receptive or empathetic, they can't access their inner feelings—unlike the women issuing the complaints, whose openness and receptiveness were central to their entire self-conception. Mayer says it was the rigid absolutism of these characterizations of men that drew her attention, and also the sheer repetitiveness; something seemed a little false about it. Men have no insides! Everything's external with them! In other words, the obverse of classic male castration anxiety—you remember, the old story that *girls* are incomplete in some way, because the boy's reaction to discovering that girls don't have penises is the unconscious fear that he might lose his too. Mayer's women patients were describing the female version: *men* are incomplete, an incompleteness that's similarly anxiety producing, and similarly congeals into disparagement and contempt.

Out of curiosity, Mayer decided to ask women she knew who'd had boy babies about their responses to diapering a boy.

She heard all about techniques for not getting sprayed, but when she probed further, several women described their initial surprise at how closed up and sealed over the babies were behind their testicles—as if they were missing an opening that should have been there. (The title of Mayer's report on the development: " 'Everybody Must Be Just Like Me.' ") This propensity to search for an *opening* resonated with the way the women described their husbands and boyfriends on an emotional level. "Sam is just incomprehensible to me," complains one wife. "He has no insides! He can't ever talk about his feelings. It's always on the outside with him."

These demands that men be more emotionally available and receptive get their force from shifts in the wider culture, Mayer supposes: this is all taking place in a context where traditional distinctions between masculinity and femininity are under assault. It starts to look as though new stereotypes are being invented to replace old stereotypes. Obviously the "men are closed up" complaint also plays on the anatomical differences between the sexes, and solidifies them as an operative metaphor: he doesn't have an opening, a route inside, he's sealed over and impossible *to get through to*—so how can he love and be receptive? But Mayer also reads an element of self-doubt behind the question: "Could I lose that capacity too?" The irony, of course, is that the worry becomes self-fulfilling: amid all these accusations and disappointments, how could love flourish?

It's the psyche's job to transform the body into metaphors that encapsulate social relations, particularly when it comes to social hierarchies, anthropologists have observed. So have historians: consider ancient Greece, where sexual penetration was only considered a "natural" sex act when it accurately represented the social hierarchy. Penetration created inferior status, so only social inferiors could be penetrated: boys, women, slaves; anything else was considered unnatural. (It's possible that this idea lingers.) New bodily metaphors arise as required, but it doesn't mean that the old metaphors just die off. As we see: even if men currently fail at openness, women don't yet seem to succeed at completeness. Having the sexual organs you've been assigned obviously isn't exactly a negligible part of inner life when we're all dragooned into living out the prevailing bodily metaphors as if they were eternal truths, and experiencing them as our deepest inner realities.

And would there be any corresponding forms of *female* avoidance or failures of openness at the moment, any questions whose answers might be uncomfortable to hear—or are men the only gender for whom self-knowledge occasionally proves elusive, the only ones who cling to compensatory stories about what's wrong with the other sex? Take scorn for men, that post-feminist badge of female independence. Can this ever be an entirely good-faith enterprise when what is this scorn but a mask for disappointment, which is to say nothing if not an index of dependency? The venerable scenario: men have the goods (commitment, attention, rings . . .) but can't or won't deliver; women need men, but are loath to admit it, wrapping denial in disparagement, whether of individual men or the sex as a whole.

The term "misogyny" has often been proffered to explain the

historic male-female predicament. But to be honest, are women really so fond of men at the moment either? Clearly when it comes to compulsively deprecating the other sex, men no longer have a monopoly: the leitmotif of today's "You go, girl" sisterhood is blanket scorn for the male sex. Just from reading the title of Maureen Dowd's 2005 best seller *Are Men Necessary? When Sexes Collide* you learn most of what you need to know about the current attitude, which is that the variety of ways women can find to dislike men are vast, and few men escape indictment for long. To begin with, every individual man bears responsibility for the oppressions of the centuries, even if temporary exemptions may be made for individual male candidates with whom you're in love or lust at the moment—that is, until he commits some form of typically male inconsideration or failure, which he eventually will. After all, he's a man! When it comes to dating, single men are dogs, infants, sex obsessed, moral rodents, or emotional incompetents. When it comes to marriage, husbands are morons, selfish, workaholics, or emotionally and domestically incompetent. Single men lie and mislead to get sex; husbands have lost interest in sex entirely. All men are inherently violent; men are all looking for a mother. Men don't express their feelings; men won't stop talking about themselves. Men are powermongers; men are wimps (what man could endure childbirth!). And so on. Pollsters attempting to quantify the rise in female dissatisfaction with men report that in 1970, 32 percent of American women said that most men are basically selfish and self-centered; in 1989, it was up to 42 percent. A 1993 Gallup poll reported that 40 percent of women were often or very resentful of men because of "irritating and just typically male behavior." Only 20 percent of men felt the same way about "typically female" behavior. Researchers who study men's attitudes about sex now generally find much higher levels of rage among women toward men than among men toward women.

As masculine failure mounts, female disappointment builds—though at least there are the consolations of female solidarity, meaning that when a woman vents about a man, another woman will invariably cheer her on with her own tale of frustration or disappointment, a comforting female-bonding ritual. (*Are Men Necessary?* was the print equivalent.) What's problematic about women's scorn for men isn't that it's necessarily undeserved, it's that it's so steeped in disavowal. Disavowal not only takes a lot of useless intellectual effort that could be devoted to other things, but is self-deceiving. Self-deception is deforming.

Q: What *is* this crucial quantity men are meant to supply, to plug up those fissures in female well-being? A: Whatever's being asked of them at the moment. Which is to say: *more* commitment, *more* sensitivity, *more* "I love you"s; *more* housework, togetherness, attention . . . What do women want from men? *More.*

Yes, relations between the sexes at the moment do have many of us flummoxed. But it's not our fault! For one thing, the whole economic substructure is shifting under our feet. Women's mass expedition into the workforce has been the fundamental social revolution of our time, radically redefining everything related to gender. Expectations of each other are in disarray. Paychecks in hand, women can afford to be more "demanding"; thus mutual irritation and new kinds of competition and uncertainty pervade the scene. Everyone's scrambling to wrest some corner of personal satisfaction from the situation and assuage the accompanying anxieties. If the favored method involves projecting those anxieties and dissatisfactions onto the opposite sex . . . well, who better?

Male-female relationships can be an agonized business, yet it's still the female half of the equation that's most willing to plunk down hard cash in hopes of salvaging things. Relationship-advice-dispensing tomes aimed at women are a staple on best-seller lists; male equivalents are strangely sparse. (Men *will* purchase self-help books, as long as they're about making more money or getting in touch with their inner golf game.) But it's not exactly an even playing field here either, as word around town is that we're facing a disastrous resource shortage: not honesty from our national leaders, not a pair of strappy sandals that don't cut into your feet like a dozen knives, but single heterosexual men wishing to couple on a long-term basis. It's not just that demand exceeds supply but also that the majority of single men are— according to field reports from those who've hazarded dating them—"relationship-challenged": in flight from commitment, their true feelings, *real* women. (And with all that porn available, the market for real women shrinks by the minute.) Thus it falls to the intimacy-seeking female to blockade the escape routes and *lure* those men out of ambivalence and into domesticity, this requiring her entry into the arcane kabbalistic world of secret knowledge possessed by only a few high priests and priestesses of the hunt: relationship experts. (Warning: extensive exposure to bullet points has been known to cause permanent cognitive impairment; read at your own risk.)

Please tell us, wise advice-book author: How's a girl supposed to nab (then restrain) one of these elusive, exit-eyeing males? Let's say you've met this guy at a party and you really seem to hit it off, and he seems *really* interested. You give him your number, but *he doesn't call.* You're *so bummed!* Should you call him? Why can't *you* make the first move—maybe he's just, you know, *shy.* Because what does gender progress amount to if women still can't call men!

Obviously you can call a man—it's the twenty-first century! Men and women are sexual equals! It's just that you don't want him to think you're *desperate.* Be strategic. Remember, men like the thrill of the chase, and if you're chasing *him,* what reason is there for him to chase *you?* You have to play hard to get (but not *too* hard). Don't be needy (but not *too* independent). Try being more of a bitch (men *love* it, really). Let him see who you really *are*—except for the part about reading advice books on how to nab a man while not appearing desperate. If he doesn't call, he doesn't deserve you! But if he does, quick, invent somewhere exciting that you're rushing off to—after all, you have a life too, a great life! In fact, why *aren't* you rushing off to someplace exciting? Maybe you aren't *putting yourself out there* enough, which is why you're at home waiting for this ambivalent loser to call you and reading advice books. By the way, is he actually *into you,* or is that wishful thinking? Wasn't that what happened the last time, when you got all goopy over Mr. I Need My Independence, who basically treated you like Booty-Call Betty? Not having had a date in a year and a half is no reason to act like a doormat; remember, you're *hot!* Here are ten bedroom tricks that *really* turn a guy on. What about an edible thong? But remember that hotness comes from *within.* It comes from self-confidence and *liking yourself.* Consider whether you may be doing something that's putting potential dates off: Is this something you should examine? Remember, we all transmit subconscious messages and cues that others respond to. Could *you* be sabotaging your love life? Lots of girls do, *without even knowing it.* Take this quiz to find out. And here's an easy way to firm your butt in just ten minutes a day—have you looked in a three-way mirror lately? But just remember, you're *foxy.*

Thanks for the . . . advice.

The irony is that even women who really *don't* want a man— don't want them as boyfriends or husbands or sex partners— usually still want *something* that men have: their salaries, for one thing, or their social privileges, or their access to those coveted corridors of power. Even proclaiming "independence" from men invariably ends up steeped in defensive posturing, since proclaiming it doesn't exactly eliminate men from the equation— not as long as they're the benchmark for achievement and equality.

Whether it's wanting to have a man or have what men *have* . . . they're still so darn central to everything, not only in the external world of social reality, but (possibly more to the point) in internal female reality as well.

Backtrack a couple of hundred years. Some revolutions were fought, democratic citizenship was established, a few freethinkers in Europe said, Hey, how about some inalienable human rights for the ladies ("a hyena in petticoats" was the response to Mary Wollstonecraft), the notion of equal rights spread, the slaves were freed, American women wanted a piece of the action too: Hey, how about some enfranchisement for *us*? Some constitutional reforms, some social reforms, some workplace reforms . . . And here we are.

Not to say that the give-us-our-rights business has been settled exactly. With men as the yardstick for social equality, yet another big missing "something" for women these days is pay equity with them. Pay equity is the one issue that most women, feminists and nonfeminists alike, can mostly agree on. Women still make 20 percent less than men, according to the latest Labor Department calculations; this is up from 38 percent less twenty-five years ago, though not yet what you'd call economic *equality*.*

But even if feminism often gets the credit (or the blame) for

*According to the AFL-CIO, the average twenty-five-year-old woman will lose almost a half-million dollars over her working life because of the wage gap.

propelling women out of the kitchen and into the job market, let's give credit where it's due: the changing needs of capital in the new information economy meant the need for new kinds of workers, and women were an available labor pool—also a cheaper one. Still, how useful to have all those upbeat catch-phrases about *female empowerment* floating around the culture just when the job market needed that influx of female labor. Note that the simmering female resentment of men proved advantageous here too: especially if women wanted what men *had,* like their jobs and their corner offices—even for lower pay.

The only problem with making pay equity the big do-or-die issue is that "equity" can just mean being equally screwed over—as it has for the middle classes. At least that's how it looks in retrospect, since, as the story unfolds, it turns out that while women did gain some economic ground over the last twenty-five years, men lost it—in absolute terms, not just relative to women. Louis Uchitelle, writing in the *New York Times,* points out that men's wages stagnated or dropped during the same period that women's rose. In other words, women's wages are up to 80 percent of men's *because* male wages are down, which evens things out. It looks as though the dirty little economic secret of the last thirty years was that the job market played women off against men to depress pay—though this shouldn't come as news to anyone, since at the moment we can watch the same dynamic unfolding on a global scale, with cheaper labor abroad used to punish overly demanding workers at home.

But even if pay equity between men and women is eventually

achieved, does this actually amount to more emancipation for anyone? Not to be a stickler, but it *was* supposed to be a liberation movement. If it turns out that pay equity can be attained without bettering anyone's quality of life—which it certainly can if "equity" ends up underwriting givebacks in the labor sphere—was this the savviest of demands? Perhaps not, or not when "equity" is confined to the sphere of gender alone. Note that during the period under discussion, we also saw major shifts in wealth and income distribution—upward that is. *All* proceeds from economic growth and increases in productivity were kicked upstairs, to the top 1 percent of households (who managed to acquire 57.5 percent of corporate wealth by 2003); the middle classes saw no gains at all. In fact, the wealth of every group other than the top 1 percent has declined since 1991. Hey, where's the equity in that? Economic inequity has *vastly* increased, with the most vulnerable segments of the middle class chucked from middle-class lifestyles and abandoned to their fates, since the traditional safety nets were also being chucked; tax policies made the wealthy wealthier and CEO salaries rose to a thousand times the average pay. Of course, the average pay would be a lot lower if the average American weren't now working an extra month a year—160 hours—compared to twenty-five years ago.

So here's a tough question: Did empowerment feminism end up playing the unwitting shill for the scorched-earth labor practices of the new global economy? As employers lopped off highly paid guys at the top and replaced them with lower-paid women, it created "a backdoor route to wage equality," says labor economist Barbara Bergmann, quoted by Uchitelle. Though this "may not be the most desirable path," and while Bergmann would prefer that pay converge in a strong economy, "however it happens, we should be happy it is happening." But . . . should we? Historically speaking, it's capitalism that's the beneficiary of internal strife within the labor force—ethnic or racial divisions function to keep wages and labor demands down. Now we've learned that sexual divisions can work the same way. The glee factor about backdoor wage equality seems open to question: after all, it's not just men who get battered in the new economy.

But eyes on the prize, wanting all that *stuff* that men supposedly have, decked out in power suits and power pumps and armed with those empowerment credos, ambitious career gals spent the last few decades flocking to leadership and networking seminars on how to become one of those mighty CEOs. A handful succeeded—some 2 percent of the biggest corporations are now run by women, the poster girls for gender progress. And how's it going for these success stories? Amid all the buzz about independence and empowerment, it seems that a few are starting to notice that they won the right to put in sixty-plus hours a week on dronelike corporate treadmills, with the full measure of accompanying stress and alienation. Now we're hearing all about low retention rates and the dissatisfaction of executive women with the managerial positions they were scraping their way into a decade or two ago—although Claudia Deutsch, writing in the *New York Times* ("Behind the Exodus of

Executive Women: Boredom"), challenges the usual explanations for women quitting the executive suites. No, it's *not* job discrimination and home-life pressures anymore, according to Deutsch. It's the "What's it all about?" question among women at the top, and frustration with the quality of their lives. "Men will grit their teeth and bear everything, while women will say: 'Is this all there is? I need more than this!' " according to Mabel Miguel, a management professor quoted by Deutsch.

So back to the old issue of *more:* clearly it's the crucial question. Still on the drawing board is what form of *more* it could be, especially if the magic kingdom of job equity doesn't look quite as alluring once you get there. At least not given the way most jobs are currently structured. (Not many people feel underworked.)

But let's not forget all the non-poster girls in the workforce, since most of the new jobs were low-end service sector positions, meaning that the majority of working women are enjoying possibly even less satisfaction and security than husbands once provided, given the increasing uncertainties of the labor situation these days: benefits down, health costs up, shrinking job security, longer periods of unemployment, and so on. As Berkeley sociologist Neil Gilbert points out a little depressingly, women may now have increasing independence from men, but what this really means is not exactly "independence," but shifting the dependency from husbands to the vagaries of the job market: to bosses, customers, and time clocks. Not that there aren't all sorts of exciting new opportunities for the financially independent women too. Let's see: there's the right to pay half the check (before pay equity has been achieved *or* equity on who calls for a second date), the right to have kids *and* work full-time (without affordable day care), and the right to pay alimony if you out-earn your husband and things don't work out (not unlikely).

So who actually gained over the last thirty years, the heyday of women's much-vaunted expedition into the workforce? As we see, the job market proved flexible enough to absorb women into its ranks with barely a hiccup, while suppressing salaries and quashing labor demands across the board. The exhilarating women's lib notion that women entering positions of economic and political power would somehow transform the character of existing social institutions turned out to be just wrong. With hindsight, the question is whether something got left out of the political calculation along the way—quality-of-life issues, for instance. Or what kind of equity to aspire to. But then why be surprised that feminism too succumbed to the winner-take-all logic of a winner-take-all economy with the oppositional edges smoothed down to suit the times. Who doesn't want to be a winner?*

As the contradictions continue to mount, now we hear that the *real* radicals are the crop of twenty-something Ivy-educated

---

*For the backstory on the backing down, consult Alice Echols's *Daring to Be Bad: Radical Feminism in America, 1967–75* on the break between feminists and the New Left, and the factionalism between liberal, socialist, and radical wings of the emerging women's movement, all of which set the direction for future political calculations.

women leading the so-called opt-out revolution, which is the new code for moms staying at home with the kids instead of ascending the career track. This is being presented as the brave new thing, with words like "choice" lobbed around just to twist the knife a little deeper for cranky old feminists, who used the word rather differently. Somehow, as highly educated as these girls are, they don't seem to have heard about the 50 percent divorce rate! Somehow, they imagine that their husbands' incomes—and loyalties—come with lifetime guarantees, thus no contingency plans for self-sufficiency will prove necessary! Let's hope they're right. (Somewhere Betty Friedan must be cackling—though recall that Friedan wrote before the advent of Prozac, which might have made all the difference for her generation of depressed stay-at-home moms, as we hope it will for their successors.)

But there's good news too. If it seems like a desirable thing for men to be more like women—you know, more *vulnerable*, more *open*—who knew that the economy would do the job for us? With status loss for men just around the next corner or the next downturn—layoffs and hiring fluctuations hit men harder than women since they still predominate in industries subject to downturns—it starts to seem like gender equality may not have to mean liberating women, it may just mean redistributing vulnerability more equally between the sexes. Between downsizing, vanishing retirement funds, corporations defaulting on pension obligations—say hello to the new male vulnerability. Economically and otherwise: you read a lot these days about the increase in male plastic surgery, men getting facials and doing their eyebrows, an upswing in male eating disorders . . . Vulnerable, self-conscious, body-obsessed: Are men the new women?

Back to the interpersonal sphere. *Dear Answer Girlfriend: I make more money than my husband does, and he's constantly making little "jokes" about it. Also our sex life has sort of, well . . . tapered off lately. I mean, it's been months! Do you think he feels emasculated? Help, what should I do? Signed, Horny in Houston.*

With women's increasing financial independence from men, and men's increasing financial feminization, we arrive at a major turning point in male-female relations: Minus economic dependency, what exactly *is* the nature of the heterosexual compact these days? No one knows anymore, and sexual anxiety runs rampant.

If there's a desperate quality to female femininity these days—the fake balloonlike tits and baby-doll drag—does it have something to do with the fact that the social glue that's supposed to hold things in place between the sexes, namely the institution of marriage, provides less and less adhesion? (The higher female earnings are, the greater the number of divorces in industrial countries, by the way.) High divorce rates leave armies of newly single middle-aged women patrolling the pickup bars and Internet dating sites of the nation and, despite their best efforts, a lot less likely to remarry than their divorced male counterparts. Scarcity produces anxiety, requiring recourse to ever more extreme strategies. The latest: extreme makeovers, extreme plastic surgeries—and consider having yours done on national television! Yes, it's the latest grisly spectator sport: in our Colosseum, the victims aren't thrown to lions, they throw themselves to cosmetic surgeons.

It remains to be seen whether extensive surgical alterations will improve relations between the sexes. But if women typically project a sense of *incompletion* onto men at the moment, and men typically project a fear of *entrapment* onto women at the moment, consider the social context: a win-lose economy, an unresponsive political system, diminishing social returns— wouldn't pretty much anyone with a central nervous system be feeling unfulfilled and trapped or dissatisfied and vulnerable? Maybe we expect so much from the opposite sex these days because we get too little everywhere else? A 2005 Wall Street Journal/NBC poll showed what the pollsters called "an angry electorate"—the majority of voters think that politicians pay too little attention to their concerns. Yet, like peeved spouses, we keep crawling back to them anyway, stewing all the way. Living in a society that's so cavalier about the basic needs of the majority does create a certain amount of emotional fallout. If only the polity of complaining women and fleeing men were issuing more ultimatums about the deteriorating conditions of collective social life, instead of confining them to the insufficiencies of the opposite sex.

It's easy to think that the upswing in body alterations has something to do with the fact that everything else you might want to change seems so intractable. Speaking of which, if you want to get a roomful of go-getting modern women really mad, just utter the magic phrase "Anatomy is destiny," then stand back, since here's where the story gets even more complicated.

Let's be frank: women just got a bad hand in the poker game of sex assignment, biologically speaking. Beneath all those rousing female empowerment slogans ("I am Woman, hear me roar"), and the table turning (*"Men* are really the weaker sex!"), and the power-suit bravado (publishing titan Judith Regan: "I have the biggest cock in the building"), there are certain anatomical facts to contend with. The degree to which these anatomical facts prop up the social inequities of gender is a long, entangled story, to say the least, and nowhere more entangled than within the female psyche itself. Like it or not, you're assigned to a gender based on what's between your legs, and for some entirely mysterious reason, in every known culture, the fact of having or not having a penis predicts who gets the economic power, social privilege, and political control. Yes, rather inexplicably (especially to those of us without one!), the majority of the advantages in the world just *seem* to accrue to the class of humans possessing this appendage. Just some zany coincidence? Vexing and absurd though all this may be, thus far in the course of human history it's a social fact (a few long-ago putative matriarchies aside), though yes, things have improved incrementally on the gender-equity front, at least in certain regions of the globe. Though not entirely.

And how does the female psyche contend with this cheery news? Well, there's the social-protest route, since obviously the female condition *is* just wrong. Or there's the old standby, femininity: that is to say, one can endeavor to acquire one of these crucial appendages on a time-share basis—otherwise known as heterosexuality, "pair-bonding," or in its legally contractual form, marriage: the system by which a few of those social and economic penis privileges are supposed to trickle down to women and their offspring. To those pursuing this option: strive to be eye-catching and tractable; try to keep the desperation concealed. Also, do keep in mind the downside of these time-share penises, which is that they invariably come with actual men attached to them—often large, messy, demanding ones, which produces for many women (especially those of us with more refined sensibilities) no end of annoyance, that is, once you finally manage to corral one of these specimens and set up housekeeping. Hence the popularity of "male behavior modification," a favorite female pastime, though rather less popular with its subjects. Studies have shown that with years of dedicated daily instruction and a structured system of punishments and rewards, a majority of men *can* learn to put the toilet seat down, so don't give up yet. (That toilet seats stand in for all domestic difficulty between the sexes doesn't seem coincidental.)

It's sometimes been suggested that lacking the body part that confers social advantage puts the female sex, on the whole, in a slightly *resentful* position, which may occasionally express itself in a degree of "overmanagement" when it comes to such domestic interactions, or a heightened focus on trivialities, as if small things mattered . . . enormously. This is, needless to say, a scurrilous stereotype, though who wouldn't be resentful about being handed the anatomical short straw, so to speak, at least until the happy day when having a shorter straw *finally stops mattering,* a day that has not quite arrived, despite all the wonderful social progress and everything. But as long as anatomy is still enlisted as the emblem of differences between the sexes, and as long as those differences are inscribed so deeply onto the female psyche, with "something's missing" as the psychological substrata of so *many* aspects of everyday life, from body image to relationships to work, perhaps even to the shape of feminism itself, the question about gender progress—to paraphrase the saying about psychoanalysis—is whether the disease and the cure begin to look in certain ways awfully similar, you know, like an aging dog owner and her aging dachshund.

When it comes to these elements of the female condition, Nietzsche's term "ressentiment" comes in handy. Basically it's a story about projecting the pain and frustration that accompanies feelings of inferiority onto some external scapegoat. Men, for instance. (Not to let them off the hook either.) You denounce the source of your pain but still want what he *has,* or at least you think you do, which creates a sort of perverse psychological bond. Only the scorn is an imaginary revenge at best—a way of escaping your own self-hatred, which you fling outward, onto the one whose presence makes you feel inferior, the supposed cause of all your frustrations. It's all rather joyless, though also infinitely reassuring, since invariably an element of self-congratulation creeps in, a lovely moral superiority.

Is it possible to advance the female cause without the scape-goating? It's quite a dilemma. Nietzsche's advice: Don't take your enemies too seriously—or if you do, keep in mind that it just binds you to them all the more ardently. But who knows this better than women!

2

SEX

An update from the front lines of the battle for male-female sexual equality: Charlotte, a thirty-year-old full-time mother from Essex, is having orgasm difficulties. So we learn from the voyeuristically fascinating British reality-TV series *Sex Inspectors*, imported to the United States in 2005. The premise of *Sex Inspectors* is this: an intrepid male-female team of real-life sex therapists locates couples with bad sex lives, installs mini–surveillance cameras around their homes, and studies how they have (or don't have) sex; then the therapists tutor the couples on the techniques and fix-its required to achieve mutual transcendence. It's the latest form of televised makeover: plastic surgery for your sagging sex life.

And what sexual obstacle do we encounter in the very first episode? Charlotte, a striking blonde who resembles the young Britt Ekland, has recently confessed to her live-in partner, Jamie, an equally telegenic building contractor, that she's been faking orgasms four or five times a week—that is, for the entirety of their year-and-a-half relationship. Charlotte and Jamie are hardly alone, according to informative stats that pop up on our screens between segments of fuzzy soft-core surveillance footage of the sexually impeded couple: 92 percent of British women admit to faking an orgasm at least once in their life. (Note to the other Sarah Bernhardts in the vicinity: Hey girlfriend, aren't you just validating men to become even *worse* lovers and really ruining things for the next bedmate who comes along? At least that's what irate female nonfakers charge when the subject arises, orgasms having become something of a political wedge issue in the sexual sisterhood these days.)

Jamie, an upbeat type, takes Charlotte's announcement in stride: "We still have a great sex life, but one of us isn't coming and the other one is."

Charlotte's problem, it seems, is twofold: she can't manage to have an orgasm through (or apparently during) penetration, which leaves her feeling frustrated and sexually insufficient; additionally, she exhibits frequent "shame behavior," according to the therapists studying her sexual performance on their tapes. Jamie's nonpenetrative sexual ministrations—namely, oral sex— do produce the desired results, but Charlotte regards this as a faulty route to feminine pleasure. She wants to have orgasms the *womanly* way: during penetration, even though the therapists assure her that some 75 percent of women don't. "She's a little bubble of insecurity," diagnoses the perky female half of the therapeutic duo, studiously regarding a taped oral sex interlude featuring Charlotte hiding her head under a pillow while Jamie burrows away.

An assortment of helpful solutions are proposed. Both couple members are coached on the mechanics of various advanced sex techniques and implements, some of which require anatomical diagrams and batteries. Charlotte gets instruction in more "partner-friendly" masturbation procedures (scatter photos of Jamie around the bed, then proceed in a face-up position, without burying her head under that sheltering pillow), thus preparing her to have orgasms with her partner in the same room, rather than her usual method of going the solo route behind closed doors. Jamie is hauled off to a manicurist (construction work *is* hard on the hands); the couple must watch less TV (only after successful sex, as a reward—like pigeons who get a pellet after pecking the correct lever in one of Skinner's behavioral conditioning experiments); they must compromise on when to have sex (Charlotte isn't a morning person; Jamie is); and, most of all, Charlotte must get over that lingering sexual shame. The solutions offered do veer toward the Skinnerian: shame is a set of behaviors that can be easily modified. Thankfully it doesn't go any deeper than that.

As we know, with the advent of the Pill in 1960, sexual revolution raged in the Western world. Women had already been practicing birth control for some time—in fact, throughout recorded history, though not always entirely successfully: the crocodile-dung barrier techniques of 1850 B.C. had a regrettably high failure rate, as did the sponges, douches, and other optimistic methods that followed. With the threat of pregnancy finally more or less abolished, the possibilities for reinventing female sexuality seemed highly promising: sexual equality all around! Spread 'em, girls! Sadly, the buoyancy proved a bit premature, and four decades of sexual emancipation later we still find a surprisingly high percentage of *sexual dissatisfaction* on the gal side of the equation, or so sexologists tell us. You even hear noises about the Pill having emancipated *men*, not *women*, letting guys off the hook for the consequences of their sexual behavior (not that such a high degree of male responsibility could really ever be counted on, as the legions of abandoned pregnant females over the course of history would no doubt attest). You hear similar complaints about the Sexual Revolution itself: maybe this wasn't really "our" revolution.

And possibly it wasn't: read through accounts of contemporary female sexual experience and you will find, in women's answers to questions about their orgasms (or lack of, more to the point), a profusion of sentiments like "unfulfilled," "angry," "robbed," "frustrated," "cheated," "resentful," "bitter," "guilty," "pissed off," "infuriated," "shortchanged," "terribly built up," "slighted," "inadequate," "upset," "climbing the wall," "in pain," "confused," "along for the ride," "I keep trying," "so frustrated that I am seriously considering getting a divorce," and "during eighteen years of marriage we did everything but stand on our heads, but there were few orgasms for me" (from *The Hite Report: A Nationwide Study of Female Sexuality*). More recent studies still put the number of women who don't consistently have orgasms as high as 58 percent, which may account for the rather adversarial tone in the air: "He always has one, so why shouldn't I?" (*Hite* again.) Unfortunately things are never very simple when it comes to female sexuality. On the one hand, women resent men for a persistent orgasm differential between the sexes; on the other, women are equally capable of resenting men for the implicit pressure to churn out orgasms when they're not forthcoming—who wants to perform on command like some kind of trained seal?

After a lot of cross-cultural globe-trotting, anthropologist Margaret Mead decided that the potential for female orgasms was entirely a cultural factor. In societies where having them was considered important, the essential techniques necessary to generate them were learned and practiced; when female orgasms were considered nonessential—or nonexistent—the techniques weren't practiced and women weren't likely to have them. By this logic, and on the evidence of recent cultural artifacts like *Sex Inspectors*, we amateur anthropologists will infer that our own culture *has* designated the female orgasm as socially important at the moment, possibly even vital. Thank you! Yes indeed, what a lot of attention female orgasms receive these days: a starring role in women's aspirations for gender equality. Parity in sexual pleasure isn't just a matter of personal fulfillment or sexual intimacy; orgasms have become an index of female progress. You might even say they've achieved the status of a radical political demand—or as much of a radical political demand as can be envisioned in the current configuration.

But culture aside, let's be honest: Nature herself has not been entirely kind to women in this regard, or less kind than to men anyway. No one likes to say this, for obvious reasons (it's kind of a downer), but among Nature's little jokes at women's expense are the entire excruciating, immobilizing burden (sorry, "privilege") of childbearing (a privilege that can kill you, thanks), PMS, painful sexual initiation . . . and on top of all that, the unkindest joke of all: the placement of the clitoris, the primary locale of female sexual pleasure, at some remove from the vagina, the primary locale of human sexual intercourse. While not an insurmountable obstacle, some percentage of the male population has yet to fathom these female anatomical complexities, despite the ongoing education efforts. And *why* were the organs of sexual pleasure and those of sexual intercourse not combined into one efficient package, as with the lucky male? Alas, we'll never know, but think how different everything might have been.

As it stands, female sexual pleasure has been one of human history's ongoing snaggles. Even in our own sexually enlightened times, there's no shortage of confusion, in practice and in theory. Just consider the conceptual problems female orgasm poses for sociobiologists and evolutionary psychologists, the go-to guys of the moment when it comes to thorny questions about human nature and gender roles. This is the crowd who likes to tell us how men and women got to be who they are (and will undoubtedly remain), by supplying colorful stories about the mating habits of our hominid ancestors and selected members of the animal kingdom.* Yet even they, usually so

---

*In the manner of Kipling's *Just So Stories* for children—"How the Camel Got His Hump," "How the Rhinoceros Got His Skin"—though with a pop-Darwinist

brimming with certainty, are at a loss when it comes to female orgasms, since in this paradigm, traits with no evolutionary purpose shouldn't endure. If there's no correlation between orgasm and conception (as with the male), if it serves no adaptive purpose, what's the point of it? And how can it be adaptive for women to have *better* orgasms in nonprocreative acts like masturbation or oral sex, as so many report? Or, if orgasm is supposed to provide an "incentive" for women to risk their lives in pregnancy—Nature's little carrot to hoodwink hapless females into servicing the species—shouldn't the carrot be a little more readily attainable during procreative sex? (Or is it that Nature doesn't want women to enjoy sex *too* much, that crafty bitch.) The best answer they've got at the moment is that the clitoris is simply a by-product of the embryological development process in which fetuses aren't sexually differentiated until around week eight of gestation. In effect, the clitoris is a truncated penis and thus responds like one. In other words, female orgasms have no purpose whatsoever—except to fuel the propensity to enlist them to tell wildly different stories about the nature of female sexuality.

But however it all came about, at the level of lived experience, things will never be entirely sexually uncomplicated for those of us assigned a female anatomy. Woman are faced with the choice

---

gloss and this time around aimed at unwary adults. All this can be entertaining when read as social fable, even if the fables in question are calculated to ratify the most tired premises about gender: man as killer ape, woman as nurturing turtledove, and so on.

between two different "systems," as Simone de Beauvoir put it regarding the whole vagina-clitoris fiasco. Basically it's like owning one of those hybrid cars that still have a few kinks to work out as your sole source of transport: the engine shuts down unexpectedly, and even when the engine's revved, it can't always be relied on to get you where you need to go. Given "the unpredictability and nonequivalence of female orgasm with intercourse," as one expert on the subject assesses the situation (note that this is a subject demanding input from *many* experts), the uncertainty of sexual pleasure has certainly been a definitive aspect of the grand female adventure here on earth, at least with men at the helm, or not without a certain amount of pedagogy. (No . . . yes . . . no, not there, *there*.)

As if all that weren't enough, factor in the whole tedious millennial saga of female virtue, modesty, shame, repression, male ineptitude . . . in short, a cruel combo of anatomical inheritance and sexual inhibition for the gal set; a nature-culture one-two punch, right to the female pleasure principle. All the recent social concern notwithstanding.

Or is that too pessimistic? Because just as we're faced with a dual-system model when it comes to anatomy, and with the nature-culture pile-on when it comes to pleasure, we also have dual narratives to choose from when it comes to the matter of sexual equality, and women's long, courageous uphill march toward achieving it. On the one hand, we have the chirpy upbeat story: welcome to the postfeminist brave new world of double-standard-rejecting, sex-toy-wielding self-confident babes, all having Mind-blowing Sex, grabbing satisfaction wherever and whenever they choose, *just like men.* After all, *women* are the ones with the organ devoted exclusively to pleasure (the splendid clitoris, far superior to the multi-tasking penis), *women* are the ones capable of multiple orgasms, like a sexual 24-7 two-for-one sale—it's always Value Day at the multiple-orgasm store. Unlike those long-ago days of sexual repression and teeth-gritting wifely duty, today's woman *owns* her sexuality. No longer must she treat sex like a commodity to trade for other commodities—love, financial support—on the open market. Now women can have sex *entirely on their own terms.* Let's call this the Sexual Progress story, in which orgasms are the sign (and sound) of the New Female Equality.

Then we have the less cheery version: let's call this the Sexual Problem story, the one peeking out from beneath the deluge of advice books and the daytime talk shows and the depressive Chick Lit, namely that for many of these same self-confident babes tossing back Jell-O shots and going home with strangers for hot, no-strings sex, the multiple orgasms are faked, the sex isn't so ecstatic (plus half the time you get dumped afterward), and basically there's a built-in disparity to the experience, a *sexual-pleasure gap* between women and men. According to national surveys of adult sexual behavior, 75 percent of men report always having orgasms, and only 29 percent of women say the same. (The gap in romantic expectations is less quantifiable; so is the degree of sexual double standard that still pertains.) Not only haven't the orgasm stats shifted much since the days of the Kinsey Report—way back in the dark ages before the Pill and the Sexual Revolution—but indications are that the numbers stack up even worse for the younger generations. Possibly with age, at least you figure out the equipment. Somehow, even for post–Gen X females, barraged by the most explicit step-by-step sexual instructions, the orgasm gap has yet to be closed: the bodies involved seem to balk at joining the New Girl Orgasm Order. Paula Kamen, author of *Her Way: Young Women Remake the Sexual Revolution*, who aims to usher the younger generation to the summits of sexual abandon and is strenuously cheery about female sexual progress (or strives to be), nevertheless ends up telling an entirely familiar story about the old female sexual inhibition.

Interviewing twenty-something women around the country, Kamen finds a lot of women who somehow can't tell men what they want in bed because they fear scaring the guy away. Here are women who are participating enthusiastically in hookup culture—one-night stands and booty calls—but who also complain that the men involved "don't care if you're getting off or not." Yet these girls keep hooking up with them! Without even getting dinner out of it! Welcome to the new femininity—at least under the old femininity, you got taken to dinner. Younger men in particular resist all helpful suggestions and entreaties, taking these as criticism of their performance, report the girls. "Women still have a long way to go to openly acknowledge their sexual desires," concludes Kamen. Yet it turns out that men aren't the only stumbling block: a surprisingly high number of women don't have orgasms even when there *aren't* men involved—that is, with other women or solo. Hence the newly minted flurry of diagnostic acronyms sweeping the culture some forty years after the Sexual Revolution was supposed to fix all this: FSD (Female Sexual Dysfunction), SAD (Sexual Arousal Disorder), SDD (Sexual Desire Disorder), and ISD (Inhibited Sexual Desire). Yes, there are infinite gradations in the vocabulary of female frustration, like cultures with a hundred words for snow. But don't fret, as there's always something called an "emotional orgasm," which many women report experiencing, according to *The Hite Report*'s queries: an "intense emotional peak" accompanied by feelings of closeness. There's a name for someone who would call that an orgasm: female.

The annoying sexual stumbling block for women has always been the "relative inefficiency of penetration as a means of producing female orgasm"—along with its ongoing popularity as a sex act in our culture, of course. Some say the problem is just that a male model of sexuality is used to define how women should function: an "androcentric" model of sexuality prevails. Even the language we use is androcentric: as Shere Hite asks, why not say "enveloping" instead of "penetrating" regarding intercourse, for example? Historian Rachel Maines points out in *The Technology of the Orgasm* that the normal female sexual response to intercourse—which is to say, frequently a lack of response—has been falsely defined on the paradigm of a disease, with accusatory clinical terminology like "frigidity" and "hysteria" tossed in women's direction when the sex is unsatisfying.

(Maines goes as far as to wonder why women sexually desire men at all, since sexual intercourse with them often proves to be a disappointment. Apparently she hasn't gotten the word on those emotional orgasms.) These days you occasionally hear alternative terms like "selfish lover" or "couldn't find my clitoris with a flashlight and a road map" in lieu of the old frigidity story; the bad news is that whomever you decide blame, whatever *Cosmo*-style therapeutics are on offer ("How to Tell a Man What Turns You On in Bed!"), the incessant patter of advice confirms the fact that pleasure equity for women remains a bit . . . elusive. Thus the job openings for all those sexperts: doctors, psychologists, and even—according to historian Maines's investigations into the invention of the vibrator—electrical engineers.

Needless to say, the sexual-pleasure gap isn't exactly a *new* problem for femalekind. The rather startling aspect of Maines's research is the evidence she's uncovered that throughout history, virtually every society has had to come up with some form of "treatment" for this fundamental female dilemma—and that for much of history, the sexual therapeutics didn't come only in the form of advice books. Until rather recently the cures were rather, if you will, *hands-on*. Female-orgasm scarcity was regarded as a medical issue and "genital massage to orgasm" was offered as a staple medical treatment, throughout the centuries, performed by physicians or midwives to relieve almost any female ailment or complaint a lady came in with. As far back as the Hippocratic corpus in the fifth century B.C. and in the medical texts of every century since, up until the early twentieth, doctors were instructed on how to manually bring women to orgasm (or to "the paroxysm," in the words of a 1653 medical compendium). Such therapies remained popular until the 1920s, providing a lucrative income stream for doctors. But despite our automatic modern suspicions about male lasciviousness under the guise of medical posturing, it doesn't appear that the doctors were particularly enjoying this task: all evidence suggests that they found it a tedious, often difficult, and labor-intensive chore. Of course, the word is that prostitutes don't much enjoy servicing their clients either; it's a job. And though Maines doesn't make the point explicitly, her narrative makes it implicitly: men have had their courtesans and hookers throughout the ages; women have had their doctors.

The reason female-orgasm production was delegated to physicians was because it was "a job nobody else wanted," in Maines's slightly sardonic phrase, especially not hapless husbands and lovers. It could take hours! It was a task far too wearisome for the ordinary man, even assuming he knew how to go about it in the first place, and clearly that couldn't be counted on.* In 1859, after having treated some 430 hysterics, a French physician named Pierre Briquet assigned the blame for the rising tide of female hysteria to *"les mauvais traitements"* of women by husbands. In other words, marital sex that lacked the desired

---

*Even now, similar tales are heard. Male comedian: "I'm really a terrible lover, I have to confess. I'm just too quick. Like the other night, my girlfriend was just starting to moan and I was already down the street at Denny's ordering a waffle."

"évacuation sexuelle" produced the need for *"la titillation du clitoris"* by physicians to relieve the multiple resulting feminine symptoms: weeping, irritability, depression, morbid fears, headaches, mental confusion, constant worry, and worse. Nevertheless, women were strongly dissuaded from taking on the job themselves, assured by medical authorities that it would impair their health and ruin their marriages. (And shrink those medical fees, of course.)

Thankfully for the worn-out doctors, the electrical vibrator was invented in the late 1880s, reducing the labor involved from hours to far more efficient sessions, often producing multiple orgasms, and reducing the fatigue factor on the part of the physician. Vibrators also required far less skill than manual massage—now doctors could service many more women in the same amount of time. Business boomed. Within fifteen years after the first electromechanical prototype was introduced by a British physician, more than a dozen models were available, both battery powered and electrical. And despite the long-standing injunctions against female masturbation, vibrators for home use were widely marketed throughout the first couple of decades of the twentieth century, advertised in women's periodicals and available through mail order—even General Electric came out with a model in 1915, touting it in full-page ads as suitable "for women's needs." Unfortunately, the fun came to an end when vibrators started showing up in stag films in the 1920s; once the medical subterfuge crumbled, vibrators fast disappeared from both the home market and doctors' offices. Happily, they would reemerge in the 1970s after a fifty-year absence, now as a badge of female sexual autonomy, along with a growing acceptance of masturbation as a self-affirming addition to the female sexual repertoire, with feminist sex gurus like Betty Dodson instructing women on advanced masturbatory techniques and the accompanying independent consciousness. "Sisters are doin' it for themselves / . . . ringing on their own bells," as Aretha Franklin sang, later covered by those emblems of female emancipation, the Spice Girls.

The medical practice of genital massage may have faded out by the 1920s, but the female orgasm was no less of a social problem. Expert ministrations were still required, though the curatives were now less direct: a vast new barrage of advice replaced assistance of the manual variety. But the purpose served by female orgasms was also shifting radically, now regarded less as a matter of hydraulics—bottled-up tension requiring release to prevent health problems—than an issue of female *identity*, the path to attaining, and performing, socially correct womanhood. From the early twentieth century to the 1970s, the prevailing sexual narrative dictated that women strive to achieve mature, more womanly "vaginal orgasms," as opposed to immature, masculine "clitoral orgasms," that wonderful Freudian contribution to deciphering the mysteries of female sexuality. Meaning that expert ministrations continued to be indispensable, as most women were not exactly sexually responsive under the new paradigm: in the 1950s the American Medical Association declared that three out of four women were frigid; others experts put it as high as 90 percent. As though things weren't difficult enough, male and female orgasms were also meant to take place simultaneously, at least on the rare occasions the latter occurred. In other words, female orgasms were now being enlisted to serve ascendant social ideals about the importance of the marital bond—say so long to the old stories about health and hysteria, and hello to companionate marriage.

By the time the 1970s rolled around, a new generation of sex experts had emerged, armed with brand-new narratives. For instance, there was Seymour Fisher, who turned the tables on the Freudian model in *Understanding the Female Orgasm* by offering an alternative way of categorizing women's personalities based on what kind of stimulation they liked. In Fisher's version, women with "high-vaginal preference"—that is, those who liked vaginal stimulation—were the new problem girls: more anxious personality types who tended to feel that their bodies were depersonalized and their orgasms not ecstatic enough. Vaginal types were more "other-directed," clitoral types more "autonomous." (Which also makes sense considering the social backdrop: as the number of women entering the job market skyrocketed in the 1970s, the autonomous clitoral type would obviously be more suited for the new economic role.) Once again, two different systems, two more chances to fail the orgasm test. Or perhaps to achieve the currently acceptable vision of proper womanhood—a girl can always dream.

Even though sexologists Masters and Johnson supposedly put the distinction between vaginal and clitoral orgasms to rest with *Human Sexual Response* in 1966, after observing hundreds of women coupling with camera-equipped artificial phalluses under laboratory conditions—and many thanks to those nameless female volunteers who sacrificed all dignity for the sake of future generations—the dual-systems issue remains entrenched in the female situation. At least it still manages to generate considerable anxiety, whether because not reaching orgasm during penetration is sexually disappointing or because men are having more of them and women are getting cheated. Shere Hite noted how much psychiatric jargon permeates women's answers to questions about sexual experience: her respondents have been well-conditioned to regard their orgasm blockages as stemming from assorted psychological "issues," particularly their ambivalences about men. Many report that they simply can't have orgasms with a penis inside them because they often dislike, distrust, or don't want to "open up to" the men on the other end of them—leading one to wonder if the fact of being in bed with them anyway indicates "issues" beyond orgasm failure alone. Hite herself prefers to blame the orgasm gap on male sexual bumbling.

This explanation has gained a certain social momentum in the intervening years. Toss out the old diagnostic vocabulary— "frigidity," "ambivalence about the female role"—because the problem is no longer women; now the problem is *men*. (Well, maybe it's also the woman's failure to effectively communicate to the guy what's sexually required of him, but that's patriarchy's fault for silencing female sexuality.) Thus a new round of grrrl-power inflected sex-advice literature is sweeping away the previous round: upbeat titles like *She Comes First: The Thinking Man's Guide to Pleasuring a Woman,* by a male sex therapist who disarmingly confesses his own past as a short-fused lover, and *The Sex You Want: A Lover's Guide to Women's Sexual Pleasure,* by two Ph.D.-wielding sisters—and by the way, what a fantasy come true a sexological sister act would have to be for that aforementioned "thinking man." *The Sex You Want* takes the sunny view that sex is learned and thus sex can also be un-learned, so even the 95 percent of heterosexuals who report that for them sex usually or always means intercourse *can* learn to have sex differently, that is, in more clitorally directed ways. Forget penetration—at least forget it for the first hour or so. *She Comes First* is similarly girl-friendly: here men learn how to identify the eighteen parts of the clitoris (undertones of a rather unappealing boy-mechanic bent here) and are led step-by-step through an array of "proven oral techniques." Stylistically, the technological vies with the cutesy in this genre: for reasons not evident—discomfort? anxiety?—bad puns abound. "Are you sex-ually cliterate?" (Ouch.) Also, the procedures in question are named after dead pop figures—the "Jackson Pollock lick," the "Elvis Presley snarl." (One fears that the thinking man isn't going to get any Ph.D.-sporting babes horizontal with limp jokes like these.)

If the nineteenth century was preoccupied with debating the question of whether women felt sexual pleasure at all—not everyone was convinced that it was advisable—in our time, the assumptions have flip-flopped. The ascendant premise is that women aren't just sexual and social equals, we're the Sex Champs, especially given the much-touted capacity for multiple orgasms, or at least we *could* be champs *if* men would get with the program. Today's female sex advice reads like a modern quest narrative: a victory over adversity in which the hero is redeemed and liberated. Our hero is the fierce and noble clitoris, waging battle with that former sexual despot, the vagina. Orgasms are, needless to say, the Holy Grail, and male ineptitude the dark forest of ignorance through which the hero must traverse. Men! If only they could find the clitoris, the blundering idiots. (Another more shadowy villain is occasionally glimpsed in the distance through foliage: female inhibition. But that's a story for another time.)

For some reason, the clitoris is always getting lost and rediscovered: throughout sexual history you find it perpetually emerging (once again) as the brand-new thing. In medieval times, when female orgasms were considered necessary for conception, the clitoris figured prominently in sexual-advice manuals. This didn't stop an Italian surgeon, Realdo Colombo, from claiming to be the first to have discovered it, in his 1559 medical treatise *De re anatomica*, where he called it the "seat of woman's delight." His critics pointed out that the clitoris had been known to medical science since the second century. More recently the clitoris gets rediscovered by Kinsey, Masters and Johnson, and Shere Hite, all enlisting it for different purposes and narratives.

Even Freud hardly ignored the existence of the thing; he just assigned it a certain role: to be outgrown. The Freudian purpose may have waned in popularity, but only because in our time the clitoris has a far more important job to do: play team leader in the battle for female sexual equity. Even if not all those in possession of a clitoris manage to hit it into the goal box every time (or, sadly, at all), who can be against the game plan?

Except then you find that women themselves have often been a little contradictory on these issues: on what sexual pleasure feels like and the important question of how you should get there. Consider the tension around what's known in the sexology trade as "manual assistance." You might think this would be just the ticket, given the dual system issue, but . . . think again. First, some background. Feminist evolutionary biologist Elisabeth Lloyd, who compiled and compared all the available studies of orgasm frequency among American and western European women (yes, now there are even studies of the studies), detected an interesting bias in them. On the question of whether women have orgasms during intercourse, the majority of studies, she soon realized, fail to distinguish between those for whom the answer is a straightforward "Yes" (20 to 24 percent) and those who require a "final push" in the form of the aforementioned manual assistance. Lloyd's point is that when these numbers *aren't* rolled together, orgasm-attainment figures are so stunningly low that they seem to imply that reaching orgasm during intercourse actually isn't *normal* for the female of the species. (Rather than deal with the implications of that for happy heterosexuality, the numbers are conveniently crunched.)

In other words, manual assistance, however prevalent in practice, is treated rather secretively by sexologists. What's more surprising is that it gets mixed reviews even among its presumed beneficiaries. Especially so, curiously, from a few of our most noted feminist thinkers and sexual iconoclasts, who've worried that such "assistance" is subtly debasing to women, maybe even creating a new kind of dependency. Simone de Beauvoir, often so lucid on female experience, was also quite a proponent of the vaginal orgasm, notwithstanding the fact that she herself had long failed to achieve them. She wrote that she had her first "real" orgasm at age forty with her lover at the time, Chicago novelist Nelson Algren (having presumably fallen short with her lifelong love, Jean-Paul Sartre, an avid sexual pursuer and, by all accounts, a terrible lover—frequently of Beauvoir's students and young gal pals). In *The Second Sex,* Beauvoir paints female sexuality as something of a no-win situation: the clitoris perpetuates juvenile independence; the vagina consigns women to the world of childbearing and economic dependency on men. The problem with clitoral stimulation—and why Beauvoir claims that many women reject it, or maybe they did in her circles—is that efforts at making a woman feel pleasure also subtly subjugate her: employing the hand is repugnant and mechanical because the hand is an instrument that doesn't participate in the pleasure it gives. Using it as an orgasm-producing tool is a feeble compensation; women end up repulsed and blocked, also dominated. Heterosexual pleasure is a pretty ambivalent experience in Beauvoir's telling: even if you manage to attain it, it's probably the wrong kind, and there goes your independence besides.

Feminist icon Germaine Greer also dismisses what she called "digital massage," deriding it as "pompous and deliberate." Greer favors a more "active" role for the vagina, which she seems to think has been slighted as an erogenous zone. Greer worries that the mission of sexual equity for women has made sex into a technocratic exercise, shaped by the alienated performance principle of the modern work world. Localizing sexual response in the clitoris makes women as sexually stunted as men: it desexualizes the rest of the body. Greer wants women to hold out not just for orgasms but for *ecstasy* (sounds good—where do you sign up?) and goes on to say that women of previous centuries didn't used to be so reticent about their vaginas as we uptight modern babes; this wisdom she gleans from two seventeenth-century bawdy ballads in which women vaunt their genitals to men, with lines like "I have a gallant Pin-box, / The like you ne'er did see" and "You'l find a Purse so deep, / You'l hardly come to the treasure." Greer somehow neglects to consider that the country lasses doing this vaunting were fictional characters and that the ballads were no doubt penned by men—a little like regarding *Behind the Green Door* as a documentary about American life in 1972 and handing out sexual advice to the rest of the girls on that basis.

Proto-feminist novelist Doris Lessing also devotes a fair amount of attention to the dual-systems issue in her 1962 novel *The Golden Notebook.* Ella, a novelist (the alter-ego of Lessing's writer-protagonist, Anna), resents her lover Paul's attempts to provide her with clitoral orgasms, which she regards as his flight from commitment and emotion. Even though the clitoral orgasms are far more powerful and thrilling, there's "only one real female orgasm and that is when a man, from the whole of his need and desire, takes a woman and wants all her response." When she informs Paul of this, he responds, "Do you know there are eminent physiologists who say women have no physical basis for vaginal orgasms?" Replies Ella, "Then they don't know much, do they?" Amid these negotiations, Paul, who happens to be a psychiatrist, relates a story about one of his female colleagues having recently walked out of a lecture by a male physician who disputed the existence of the vaginal orgasm, after which she explained to Paul, "Women of any sense know better, after all these centuries, than to interrupt when men start telling them how they feel about sex." Nevertheless, Paul still doesn't get it—his preference for clitoral orgasms becomes a sign that he's about to leave Ella, and sure enough, soon he's out the door.

If Lessing saw clitoral orgasms as something foisted on women out of male-intimacy fears, if Beauvoir and Greer worried that manual assistance cheapened sex and fostered female dependency, clearly it's not simply achieving sexual pleasure that's the issue for women; it's also achieving some kind of narrative coherence about it. Possessing one of these dual-clutch female anatomies does lend a certain duality to the whole sexual experience. At least, possessing the equipment doesn't guarantee any particular clarity on the subject; nor does being a renowned feminist. Note that in today's terms, Lessing's character Paul would be the male feminist hero, battling on behalf of the oppressed clitoris—exactly what today's busy career gal wants from a lover. Who even has *time* for vaginal orgasms any more—that is, if they exist, which as everyone now knows, they don't. Or we don't think so. At the moment. Check back next week.

Just when things couldn't seem any less cohesive on the female-pleasure front, along came another twist, the discovery of a whole *new* female erogenous zone: the "G-spot." For those who didn't get the bulletin, this is a special orgasm-producing zone in the upper vagina, first discovered by a German doctor named Ernst Grafenberg in 1950 and popularized by someone else in a 1982 eponymous best-selling sex manual. It quickly became the great female sexual hope, and so it remains. On *Sex Inspectors*, Charlotte and Jamie are introduced to it by means of a helpful anatomical diagram reminiscent of Biology 101: their TV therapists are confident that this invaluable info is the key to solving the couple's erotic problems. Unfortunately, it's an anatomical locale that's since been shown not to exist, at least according to rival sex expert Shere Hite. Or wait, does it? Possibly it's not so much a spot as an *area*. The debate rages on. Adherents tout its existence with near-religious zeal; those who doubt this or the mythic powers attributed to it are dismissed as sexual flat-earthers. Of course, if it *does* exist, what a boon— since this would be equivalent to having a clitoris *inside* the vagina instead of inconveniently located miles away (well, sometimes it seems like miles). The G-spot is basically where the clitoris *should* have been located—that is, if sexual intercourse actually made sense from the standpoint of efficient female pleasure. Or maybe it's like the emotional orgasm: if you think it exists, you're two-thirds of the way to achieving one.

But reaping the rewards requires locating the damn thing, and there's the hitch. Even for the most dedicated explorers, navigational difficulties abound—it's about as easy to track down as the source of the Nile for a blindfolded traveler. Consider a recent query on the subject directed to Dr. Hilda Hutcherson, the resident sex expert on the Oprah website. In response to an earnest seeker ("This is my first time discussing this subject with someone other than my husband. We have been trying to locate my G-spot for some time now and we just can't find it. Is it possible for you to give some direction on how to find the G-spot? What I should be feeling and experiencing with this whole situation? I would really love to know this feeling even if it's only one time."), the helpful Dr. Hilda replies:

Oh, the elusive G-spot. Many a man has, unfortunately, become lost while searching for it. Your G-spot is located on the front wall of your vagina, midway between the opening of your vagina and your cervix. This area often feels bumpy or rough. . . . *Don't be surprised if you feel no pleasure at all when you find your G-spot. Sometimes it takes multiple sessions, and some women never find pleasure from G-spot massage.* Remember, every woman is different. At the very least, you and your husband can enjoy the journey. Don't forget to look for other sensitive areas along the way. [Italics added.]

It's like going off on a safari—have a great trip, send postcards! Should you fail in your pursuit, it's not your fault; you're just another victim of the patriarchal conspiracy to suppress knowledge about female sexuality and the full extent of its power, which if ever fully unleashed would overturn civilization as we know it.* Thus the authors of *The Sex You Want* chide a questioner for wondering whether the G-spot really exists:

Most body parts are not optional. If some women have a G-spot it is likely that all women do. Many women have never looked for their G-spot because they are either unaware of it or doubt that it exists. Rather than asking whether or not all women have a G-spot, women should be asking why it remains a mystery instead of being treated as a pleasurable fact of a woman's sexual experience.

So shut up and keep digging, ladies. Should you find yourself wondering how the G-spot orgasm differs from the contemptible Freudian vaginal orgasm, quash that thought immediately. "To

---

*A common premise of second-wave feminism was that containing the power of female sexuality was necessary to preserve male hierarchy. Not foreseen was how easily commodified hot, unfettered female sexuality could be, packaged and sold back to women in the form of pricey accoutrements: the bad-girl lingerie, the kitten-with-a-whip wardrobe, the fuck-me heels, and the regular bikini waxes. No, female sexuality unleashed hasn't exactly been a nail in the coffin of capitalist patriarchy.

see the G-spot as the site of the 'vaginal' orgasm is to hand the vagina back to Freud instead of encouraging women to define its pleasures for themselves," say the *Sex You Want* authors. Got that? How great that women are finally being encouraged to define pleasure for themselves!

The hunt for the G-spot brings to mind another anatomical quest story, the 1972 porn classic *Deep Throat*, though this may seem like an odd comparison. Reportedly the most profitable movie of all time, and the first porn film seen by substantial numbers of women, *Deep Throat* became a cult viewing experience; despite (possibly because of) the schlocky acting and inane plot, audiences loved this movie. As it happens, the theme of the film is precisely the predicament under discussion: the obstacles to female orgasms and the mission to achieve them, despite anatomical hindrances. The joke is that the clitoris of its sexually frustrated protagonist, Linda, isn't just the usual problematic distance from her vagina; in her case it's even farther away. In fact, it's finally located by a helpful local physician . . . in her throat. The discovery overjoys everyone: Linda has orgasm after orgasm, rockets and fireworks go off, church bells peel, and the world is a far happier place.

Sure, it's easy to dismiss the misplaced-clitoris gag as a setup for extended fellatio scenes (or women "sexually servicing men," as antiporn arguments tend to put it), but there's also something a little wistful about the premise. It's the fantasy of an alternative bodily universe where men and women get pleasure from doing the same things, in lieu of the erotically mismatched world we've inherited, where sexual synchrony is a long shot and dissatisfaction so often the outcome. Pornography's critics take porn very literally, as if it purports to be social realism, but a better comparison would be sci-fi, another genre that takes the "what if things were different?" approach to bodies and societies. Besides, what's so great about reality anyway, and if realism can't compete with pornography, why is it porn that's supposed to do the apologizing?

Sexual synchrony between men and women—what an interesting prospect to contemplate. If sexual pleasure *were* more of a sure thing for women, what vast social and personal transformations would follow? After all, if women did have orgasms while performing oral sex, if women even had orgasms with the frequency that men do in sexual intercourse, would women finally manage to give up the tiresome female role of Sexual Gatekeeper? Consider the transformations to the female psyche this alone would entail. In fact, just such a gender transformation was one of the central fantasies of the TV series *Sex and the City*—like *Deep Throat*, also frequently criticized for its crimes against realism. (Critics protested that the main character couldn't have afforded all those designer shoes on her salary.) One character, Samantha, the aging slutty blonde, had effortless, ecstatic orgasms a hundred percent of the time, and was consequently willing to drop her drawers and have sex on the spot with any well-built guy she happened on: deliverymen, doormen, waiters—she was an equal-opportunity shagger. (Since no actual female could get this much pleasure from sex, Samantha's behavior was frequently explained in the media with reference to the show's gay producer: Samantha actually had the mind of a gay male.) But consider that the traditional version of pornography for women—the romance novel—also undertakes to reorganize the contours of gender; though in the case of romance fiction, it's men who undergo the gender transformation. The reconfigurations in the romance genre are psychological rather than anatomical: imbuing men with sensitivity and insight into female needs, like really handsome girlfriends with penises. Romance fiction is a $1.2-billion-a-year industry, well behind pornography (estimates put it at $9 billion a year), but between the two, you do get the idea that both men and women are doing a lot of fantasizing about radically transforming the other sex.*

Back on earth, whether men and women are more sexually alike or sexually different remains the fundamental question. The answer? It depends on how you tell the story. But it's no use trying to derive the solution from the body, since the body is forever being creatively reimagined in ways that ratify existing social premises about gender, including premises about whether men and women are more alike or different. In other words, believing is seeing when it comes to anatomical differences. Before the eighteenth century, the general medical belief was that women had a penis inside their bodies, according to historian

*And a lot of fetishizing. The feminist premise that men fetishize women's bodies has had a certain popularity, but it's not clear that women fetishize men any less. Romance is just a better cover story for it than porn.

Thomas Laqueur. Yes, for several thousand years, the accepted medical view was that the female body had all the same organs as the male, just located on the inside rather than the outside. In other words, women were lesser men: all the same equipment, just an inferior version of it. The vagina was an inverted penis, the ovaries were female testicles, the womb was a scrotum, and so on. Medical illustrations of the uterus looked exactly like an inside-out penis. Then, come the late eighteenth century, a whole *new* model of male-female difference emerged. Down with the premise of male-female homologies, up with a radical new premise: male and female as anatomical *opposites*. And along with the anatomical overhaul came a total revision of female capacities for sexual pleasure: in the previous model, women's sexual desires had been equivalent to men's, now female desire was regarded as completely different. In fact, as the Victorian era unfurled, it began to seem doubtful that women had sexual desire at all; the view that prevailed throughout the nineteenth century, with anatomy and medical knowledge reconfigured to support the new sexual ideology. Laqueur, whose work skewers the concept that there's anything "natural" about the body, makes this central point: *nothing* about the dramatic reinterpretation of the female body hinged on any new anatomical discoveries; the old knowledge was simply reformulated to support the new story.

It happens that this big biological shakeup took place just at the point when the foundations of the pre-Enlightenment social order were being upended in the wake of the modern era, including by feminists like Wollstonecraft, who wanted to extend the new political demands for liberty and equality to women. What begins to seem clear is that the body is always treated as an image of society: all the stories we tell about it are cultural and political narratives dressed up in an anatomical guise. New cultural narratives about women and their place in the world invariably get mapped back onto the female body and female genitals; the "scientific" concepts that support the conclusions come along later, to prop up the new story.

Fast-forward to our time. Regard the adventures of the socially ascendant clitoris. How can we not be thrilled on its behalf, transported from underdog to überorgan, even migrating from women's bodies to men's? Yes, one of the latest anatomical stories in circulation is that men *too* have clitorises. Exciting news: there's a five-inch tube-shaped sexual organ inside the penis, which the authors of *The Sex You Want* and a handful of others have named the "male clitoris," since it serves the same pleasure function as the female version. Whether you take this as an anatomy lesson or a social allegory, calling this tube a clitoris does at least reverse the dastardly Freudian story that the clitoris is an inferior penis. Forget the penis; now the clitoris is the gold standard for *all* genitals. And gosh, if men have clitorises, maybe men and women really *are* more alike than we thought. Also, have you heard the great news that women too can ejaculate, just like a man? So say G-spot proponents, who regard this ability in a highly celebratory light, a social achievement on par with ending global warming or finding a cure for herpes. Needless to say, there are dissenters, even among women: curmudgeon Germaine Greer is a naysayer on female ejaculation, proclaiming the notion "utterly fanciful." Chastises Greer: "All kinds of false ideas are still in circulation about women."

So . . . there are *true* ideas about women?

For most of history, orgasms were regarded as necessary for conception; now we have "maternal instinct" as a conception aid, and orgasms are required for gender equity. Clearly orgasms can be conscripted for all sorts of social purposes, including reparations for the gender crimes of eras past. Our forty acres and a mule; orgasm equity *can be ours.*

Childrearing equity can't, however. Once women were faced with the vaginal-orgasm-versus-clitoral-orgasm dichotomy; now women are faced with the motherhood-versus-career dichotomy. These may sound like different kinds of dilemmas, but in fact they have structural similarities, and a similar underlying logic. To begin with, we have the same cast of characters: the womanly other-directed dependent type versus the masculine-identified striving autonomous type. And in both cases, a socially organized choice masquerades as a natural one, manufacturing a big dilemma where one doesn't have to exist. The dilemma is experienced by the female involved as pertaining to the nature of her womanhood, and the quest to fulfill it, and, of course, all the various ways there are to fall short or miss out.

But what happens when we think about female sexuality as a totality: pleasure *and* pregnancy, *and* the contemporary sexual bargain, namely, Who raises the next generation? Why is it that female sexuality can be reimagined at one end of the equation but not at the other? After all, there are ways to organize society and sexuality that don't create false choices—once again, it depends how you decide to tell the story.

Consider the issue of female sexual pleasure. One available way to account for the orgasm differential between men and women is that women are just anatomically constructed in such a way that a certain amount of dissatisfaction comes with the territory, and leave it at that. The anatomy in question can obviously be enlisted to tell that story; it just doesn't happen to be the most socially favored explanation at the moment. A more palatable story is that it's society's definition of sex that's been oppressive to women, but that can *change*, because we believe it should. Men can be educated to become better lovers, women can learn to become less repressed, we can all "communicate" more—women can even sprout all sorts of new erogenous regions and capacities, because *sexual equity is our right*.

Somehow we're not quite so inventive when it comes to that other looming female duality of the moment: the motherhood-career dilemma. When it comes to maternity, those who were big culturalists a minute ago are suddenly reborn as raging biological determinists. It must be added that women themselves haven't helped much here, at least not those who go around touting that mystical feeling known as "maternal instinct," along with biological clocks, mother-infant bonds, and so on.* If biology speaks to women in a direct hookup from womb to brain, guess what—this *will* parlay into who should do the social job of childrearing. Men and women can't have childrearing equity, and day care isn't going to be a social entitlement like public education, because that's not "natural."

As with the G-spot or the male clitoris, maternal instinct is also a concept that arises at a particular point in history— namely, when there was a social necessity for a new story. With the industrial revolution, children's economic value declined: they weren't necessary additions to the household labor force, and once children started costing more to raise than they con- tributed economically to the household, there had to be *some* justification for having them. Ironically, it was only when chil- dren lost economic worth that they became the priceless little treasures we know them as today. On the emotional side, it also took a decline in infant-mortality rates for parents to start treat- ing their offspring with much affection—when infant deaths

---

*According to Diane Eyer's *Mother-Infant Bonding,* the concept that bonding has any biological basis is "scientific fictionalizing." Bonding research has been dismissed by much of the scientific community as an ideological rather than a scientific premise, Eyer says, driven by popular concepts about true woman- hood and a woman's place being in the home, concepts Eyer traces back to the rise of industrialization, when wage labor becomes an option for women. The bonding story got revved up once again in the early 1970s, just as women were moving into the labor market and screwing up cultural conceptions about the female role, popularized by child-development experts like pediatrician T. Berry Brazelton, who said that mothers who don't stay at home with children for the first year to bond spawn delinquents and terrorists.

were high (in England prior to 1800 they ran between 15 and 30 percent for a child's first year), maternal attachment ran low. (Historian Lawrence Stone points out the common practice of giving a newborn child the same name as a dead sibling: children were barely even regarded as distinct individuals.) With smaller family size—birthrates declined steeply in the nineteenth century—the emotional value of each child also increased; so did sentimentality about children and the deeply felt emotional need to acquire them.

Human maternity has had a checkered history over the ages, it must be said, including such maternal traditions as infanticide and child abandonment, sending children to wet nurses following birth and to foundling hospitals or workhouses when economic circumstances were dire ("little more than licensed death camps," says Stone). In other words, what we now like to call an "instinct" is a culturally specific development, also an economic luxury. Which isn't to say that an invented instinct *feels* any less real; it can feel entirely profound. But it does mean there's no reason it can't be invented differently—or invented in men as well—when social priorities dictate. Nevertheless, "maternal instinct" did its job: it helped explain the new industrial-era sexual division of labor, the one where men go to work and women stay home raising kids, as if such arrangements were handed down by nature. (Before the industrial revolution, everyone worked at home—the male-breadwinner family has actually only prevailed for a relatively short period.) But stand by for a late-breaking development: it turns out that the economy has new plans for women at the moment, which may mean that the old story about "female nature" will be undergoing a face-lift soon. Possibly also the one about stay-at-home moms as "what's best for the children." Try this one on for size: how much sacrificial stay-at-home mothering can one tiny human endure before requiring psychiatric intervention? But for the moment the old narratives and the New Economy continue to uneasily coexist, meaning a lot of emotional fallout for everyone: guilt, conflict, and women sniping at each other about their respective "choices."

Still, there's no getting around the fact that women have been "ensnared by nature," in Beauvoir's phrase—if it were solely up to nature, women would compliantly serve as life's passive instruments and pipe down with the social demands. It's only modern technology's role in overriding female nature—lowering the maternal death rate, inventing the Pill, and let's not forget those vibrators—that's offered women any modicum of self-determination. It's sometimes been said that the natural world isn't given sufficient credit for inspiring human tyranny; obviously that goes double for tyranny over women: technology and modernity have liberated women as much as feminism has. Inexplicably, rather a lot of women still demonstrate a weird tendency to sentimentalize Nature, like it were a special *girlfriend*—yes, *we* have a special *relationship* with the earth, the oceans, the moon . . . Not like girlfriend Nature just blithely kills off women to perpetuate the species on a random basis or anything. One of the great dissenters on the dippy Nature-hugging was radical feminist Shulamith Firestone in *The Dialectic of Sex*, who called childbirth "barbaric," said that "it isn't good for you," compared it to "shitting a pumpkin," and maintained that women won't get social equality until there's some technological solution to childbearing.

In the meantime, women may talk the talk on maternal instinct (especially when it turned out that the ruthless world of career advancement isn't a straight shot to the pinnacles of female contentment), but we're not exactly walking the walk: birthrates across the industrialized world have been in steep decline ever since the Pill. (Yes, while an overpopulation crisis looms in the developing world, underpopulation hits this part of the globe.) Women are voting with their ovaries, and they're increasingly voting No to lives devoted exclusively to maternity. Even if femalehood and motherhood are still united in the sentimental imagination, the reality is that the majority of women aren't mothers anymore, they're *mother-workers*. The fastest-growing segments of the female population now have either zero or one child by age forty, double the percentage thirty years ago; the proportion of women with only two children by age forty has increased by 75 percent. According to demographers, the consequences will be seismic down the road: an aging population unable to sustain itself economically and—some are already predicting—the eventual resort to biotechnological solutions like artificial wombs and baby farms if we modern gals can't somehow be induced to repopulate the planet by pushing out 2.1 children per uterus. Consider Japan, with one of the lowest birth rates in the world at 1.3: schools are closing, with many converting into senior centers; hospital pediatric wings are being shut down, and pediatricians are retraining as geriatric specialists; theme parks aimed at children have disappeared. Traditionally, married women stayed home to raise the kids; now 70 percent of young Japanese women say they're not interested in marriage. Some towns are even offering cash incentives for couples willing to have a baby. The United States isn't far behind, with its own Social Security drain, and its own graying population turning the national pension system into an impending national Ponzi scheme and spawning a national debate over immigration amnesty—after all, someone has to pay in to forestall the whole thing collapsing.

The lowdown on the birthrate drop-off goes like this: as if bearing all the offspring weren't service enough on behalf of the species, women are typically saddled with raising these offspring too, which is—how to put this politely?—not exactly what you'd call a socially valued activity. Thus, given sufficient monetary resources, those who can will quickly enlist other women with fewer monetary resources to raise them instead, or at least to deal with the more boring and messy parts of child-rearing, of which there are many. Yes, what a bundle of joy children can be. On the other hand, let's face it: children's intellectual capacities and conversational acumen are really not their best feature; thus boredom and intellectual atrophy are the normal conditions of daily life for the child-raising classes. Once women entered higher education in increasing numbers, once the job market opened its arms (if not its coffers), birthrates plummeted even further: women with the most education are the ones having the fewest children. But even basic literacy has a negative effect on birthrates in the developing world: the higher the literacy rate, the lower the birthrate—give a girl a book, say goodbye to overpopulation. In other words, when women acquire critical skills and start weighing their options, they quickly wise up to the fact that they've been getting a raw deal: too little social recompense for their labors. (Sorry for the pun.)

Memo to those concerned about falling birthrates: make men raise the little tykes too. In fact, the family minister of another country facing an underpopulation crisis, Germany (with one of Europe's lowest birthrates and the highest proportion of childless women), proposed a series of radical social measures in 2005, including requiring men to take two months off work to look after a newborn child if they wanted to qualify for state-funded child-welfare support, and offering parents 67 percent of their previous incomes while they stayed home with the children. Strangely, these proposals were tabled: critics derided the family minister for trying to force men to abandon work to change nappies. Fine, but then why should women? And that's the subtext of falling birthrates: think of it as a production slowdown.

Maintaining the species is something both sexes would appear to have a stake in. The work-family trade-off isn't only a female dilemma, or a product of silly "have it all" '70s feminism. But until there's a better social deal—whether that means that men do more kid duty, or well-paid professionals step in because vastly more social resources are directed at the problem—it *will* remain the case that taking on childrearing full-time immediately drops you down a few dozen rungs in the social-equity ranks. Whereas when both sexes share the childrearing, it will instantly become a more socially valued enterprise, and everyone will be far happier doing it. In the interim, notwithstanding a handful of househusbands, the solution has been the one-child family and all the demographic consequences. The one-child mom at least gets to fulfill her raging maternal instincts, though generally while performing the majority of the childrearing and most of the housework and often holding down a job too. (The have-it-alls with six-figure salaries get an easier deal, of course.) Women who have two kids generally leave their jobs to become full-time moms, according to sociologist Neil Gilbert, then attempt to reenter the workforce sometime later, when the kids are in school—good luck on that, given the existing organization of the workplace. How really appreciated you'll be when you hit the job market with a big gap in your employment record because you left the workforce to devote yourself to repopulating the nation. In the meantime, let's hope that hubby sticks around, since he's your only source of income.

By the way, do you think it's true that stay-at-home wives and off-to-work husbands have a tendency to drift apart because they live in different worlds? Consider the confession of former fast-track executive turned housebound mom Debbie Klett. Co-founder of a magazine called *Total 180!* for those in the same boat, here is Klett on forgetting how to talk to another adult after being home with the kids all day: "I remember my husband getting home one night and suggesting we get pizza. And I took down the phone book and started counting the places we could order from: 'One, two, three, four, five . . .' and he said, 'You don't have to count like that to me.' " Or maybe Mom starts to resent Dad's freedom and to nag him for not helping more when he finally gets home from work, and Dad starts staying even later at work and Mom resents him even more, which he finds himself complaining about to his attractive coworker over drinks . . . and other variations on the theme of family values.

Another question: *Is it really such a great idea to rely* on the more aggrieved sex to do all the childrearing—the sex whose emotional needs are most socially disparaged, whose labors are most undervalued, and who may consequently be a little . . . on edge? Who among us, placed in such a position, *wouldn't* seize the opportunity to exercise the power we're denied in the rest of the world over the kids? Hey, is it such a crime to use children in compensatory ways—to assuage life's disappointments, to have *something* to control and perfect?

Actually "perfection" barely describes the overdrive mothering style of today's former careerists turned full-time moms. In babies women acquire the opportunity for domination that men have historically had over women, and rename it "maternal devotion," the childless Simone de Beauvoir wrote. But it's *so* great for the kids, having Mom at home full-time, just where

Nature intended, with jurisdiction over your every need, *controlling* everything—thwarting some desires, fulfilling others. . . . The first despot in our lives, as Dorothy Dinnerstein puts it a little chillingly in *The Mermaid and the Minotaur,* an investigation into what she calls the "human malaise" of our current sexual arrangements—namely, mother-dominated childrearing. The psychological origins of misogyny are in precisely this dynamic, Dinnerstein and others have proposed. Misogyny is basically just the need for mother-raised humans to overthrow the residues of early female dominion, and men aren't going to give up ruling the world until women stop ruling over childhood. (What goes around comes around, girls.) Unfortunately, women *can't* stop ruling over childhood—because we have those maternal instincts to mollify. Also because no one else will do it, of course. It wouldn't be natural! (It also wouldn't be socially inexpensive.)

But in the meantime, thanks for the fab orgasms! Really, *thanks.*

3

DIRT

Can't you pick up your goddamn socks? Have you never heard of a hamper? Could I just for once come into the bedroom and not see your underwear on the floor? Do you think I'm your mother? Am I the only one who cares how the house looks . . .

Which sex is the dirtiest, men or women? Well, let's see. Do you leave your socks strewn wherever you happen to remove them? According to current cultural norms, you must be of the male persuasion. Do you rush to scrub the bathroom before last-minute guests descend? You are likely the female of the household. (Yes, we can all think of exceptions, but please go with me on this for a minute.) Are you the one who claims "not to notice" that the bathroom is a disgusting, scummy, hair-matted germ trap until it's pointed out to you more than once, the one who may give it a few wipes or swishes if repeatedly commanded or entreated (only after extensive instruction in the complicated mechanics of wielding a mop or toilet brush) but who performs the task haphazardly at best, often requiring a second go-around by other concerned parties? Parties who may, in consequence, begin to "lose interest" in previously mutually gratifying couple activities such as . . . sex? Ah, here's where things get even more interesting in contemporary domestic life: passive-aggressiveness makes a guest appearance, what fun for all involved. As we will see, the subject of dirt gets us into some knotty and ambivalent human terrain.

The Big Question of the day when it comes to gender progress: Why are so many women still doing a majority of the housework? Do women *gravitate* toward dirt for some unknown reason? Let's begin our inquiries with Allison Pearson's bestselling working-wife novel *I Don't Know How She Does It,* which tells just such a tale. We open with beleaguered and jet-lagged executive mom Kate Reddy cleaning the kitchen at two a.m. after returning from an overseas business trip.

> After washing and drying the bowl . . . I sniff the dishcloth. Slimy with bacteria, it has the sweet sickening stench of dead-flower water. Exactly how rancid would a dishcloth have to be before someone else in this house thought to throw it away?

Good question! Or to put it slightly differently, *can* someone—that someone being female—manage to liberate herself from her own psychological relation to dirt? The history of women's relationship with dirt is obviously rather involved (you might even say *messy*), a history not just social but often strangely emotional, in fact weighed down by all kinds of "emotional baggage." (Cleanliness and neurosis: now there's a topic.)

Housekeeping has been the assigned female occupational role for some time now—for about as long as there have been houses (the word "housewife" dates from the thirteenth century), or possibly since the invention of the plow: plowing required upper-body strength, which deflated the value of women's agricultural labor compared to men's, thus shunting the females into domestic labor, where they would remain stuck for the next few millennia and increasingly pissed off about it. But social history alone doesn't tell you the whole story about women and dirt. It doesn't tell you why large-scale social changes—women's mass expedition into the workforce, for one thing—often leave inner life behind, what sociologists like to call *role conflict*, an authoritative-sounding term that fails to shed any light whatsoever on why a woman is more prone to sniff a rancid dishcloth than her husband is.

And if contemporary women still seem generally more psychologically *attuned* to dirt than men generally seem to be, how *will* women ever really achieve social equality when even a high paid glass-ceiling-smashing corporate go-getter type like Kate Reddy somehow can't stop herself from *noticing* what needs cleaning, thus winds up in the kitchen at two a.m. frantically scrubbing things? Later we come across Kate unloading the dishwasher and rewashing by hand the plates that didn't get clean enough; then crawling the length of the hallway on her hands and knees picking up dust clumps like a human Hoover. Kate does have a cleaning woman, Juanita. Unfortunately, Juanita has a cartilage problem and can't kneel down, her vertigo prevents her from cleaning above waist level, and a chronic bad back means she's unable to tote laundry baskets. Additionally

Kate has a nanny, Paula. Paula refuses to clean up after the adults of the house, meanwhile holding them hostage to her moods. You don't need a psychology degree to discern that Kate's a woman who prefers to do her own cleaning up, while feeling a little victimized about it.

To put it bluntly, it's unclear whether the real domestic problem between the sexes is that men *won't* clean or that women *will*.

But there's also nothing new about neurotic acting out between the sexes over cleanliness. As even a casual foray through the anthropological literature will indicate, throughout the course of human society, one sex or the other is perpetually cast as the dirtier and has to pay the price in social censure and moral condemnation; this is one of our most symbolically enduring themes. In the current social mythology, men may be the ones typically assigned to this disparaged role, but in fact it's *women* who've been considered the dirtier sex for most of recorded time. All through the history of civilization, in cultures world over, accusations of dirtiness have constantly been leveled at women, with men the ones devoted to scrubbing out yucky female contamination, often armed with powerful detergents in the form of rituals, taboos, and religion (with its numerous purity rites). If modern life reverses the old pattern, apparently somewhere along the way the tables got turned in the human-dirtiness rivalry. Thus accusations of dirtiness are now continuously leveled at *men:* why can't they figure out how to wipe the counter, take out the garbage, pick up their undergarments? In fact, men are altogether more "dirty-minded" generally—we'll be getting to this. But does being the purportedly "cleaner" sex really turn out to be such a great leap forward for women? This is the fundamental question.

Which brings us to another question: *What is dirt?* This may not be as obvious as it seems. The standard definition of dirt is "matter in the wrong place," meaning that shoes on the floor are not much of an issue, but shoes on the bed cause distress; crumbs on a plate are fine, but crumbs on the floor are dirty, and so on. You begin to see that dirt is basically a conceptual issue: it depends on the categories you bring to it. But if dirt is in the eye of the beholder and cleanliness is a product of the imagination, how can there be any absolute standards, including yours, and the ones you may want to hold over those you reside with, or they over you? And where do these standards come from anyway? It's all very mysterious, like the popularity of Martha Stewart or the origin of dust. As psychoanalyst Lawrence Kubie put it in a provocative 1937 essay "The Fantasy of Dirt": "Our behavior towards things that are usually thought of as 'dirty' is replete with paradoxes, absurdities, confused assumptions, and mutually contradictory implications and premises."

Dirtiness has an inherent psychological drama to it, a drama that cuts deep into the psyche. For the fastidious, which includes all of us socialized humans at least some of the time, there's the sense of something vaguely *dangerous* about dirt. It threatens us with chaos and disorder and . . . well, who knows what exactly?

Try querying cleaning devotees about what's really so vexing about bathroom scum, why those crumbs on the counter just have to be wiped up before leaving the house, what prompts the urgent nighttime scrubbing fits, and you learn nothing, only that such impulses reside beneath the level of cogent thought, shrouded in a fuzzy blend of defensiveness and ersatz common sense. When pressed, just about everyone now rationalizes the danger feelings with authoritative-sounding concepts about disease or germs, but it's also obvious that these concepts come after the fact, to justify the anxiety that preceded the explanations.

A Kalahari Bushman believes that if a man sits on the female side of the hut his virility will be weakened. We fear pathogenicity transmitted through microorganisms. We're both marshalling our culture's version of pollution avoidance to triumph over abstract fears and dangers, because obviously the world is packed with them, they're frequently capricious and unpredictable, they hover in the anxious territory between the real and the imaginary, and so humans invent boundaries as a feeble mode of injecting some control into a phobia-inducing universe. But the joke's on us, since needless to say, the boundaries produce as many anxieties as they alleviate. Note that jokes themselves are an important anxiety-assuagement technique, especially jokes about boundaries: incest jokes, toilet jokes, bestiality jokes—try to think of a social boundary that isn't prime material for comedy. But the difference between us cosmopolitans and the Bushmen isn't that our behavior is rational and grounded in science and theirs in symbolism, because our behavior carries just as much symbolic meaning as theirs. Scrubbing things temporarily controls and orders the world, as with all forms of ritualistic behavior. The problem is that the effectiveness of the rituals is so laughably temporary.

One way of creating order is by exaggerating differences— for instance, the distinction between the sexes about which one's dirtiest. Who cares if the distinctions are irrational? Social psychologists who research disgust like to torment their subjects (usually hapless undergraduates) by conducting what they call "contamination studies"; such studies have proven conclusively that most people are unwilling to eat a bowl of their favorite soup stirred by a never-used flyswatter. Flyswatter plus soup is a profound category violation; even thinking about it can make you a little nauseous. It soon becomes evident that everything related to dirt and contamination is also hot-wired to emotions of disgust. Disgust gives rise to emotions of endangerment and vulnerability, and who likes feeling *vulnerable*?

So back to the female thing. If women are situated in the world, bodily and socially, as the more vulnerable sex, we begin to see how the social role of Happy Homemaker might capitalize on a psychological propensity, with the two becoming mutually enforcing.

But dirt is a central category for all humans because the whole concept of "dirtiness" is tied to smells and textures whose existence we generally prefer to deny—those shame-ridden bodily functions and messy body products that we civilized beings prefer to distance ourselves from. Obviously what dirt most resembles is . . . *shit*. In other words, our own bodies are the culprits when it comes to dirt. The body is "a kind of animated, mobile dirt factory, exuding filth at every aperture," Dr. Kubie informs us. This is a little distressing, and the uneasy knowledge that our bodies themselves are deeply filthy is one reason to shun anything that reminds us of our own essentially contaminated condition.

Thus your primary human hygiene task is not to let your relatively clean "outside"—that is, the skin—become contaminated by its own filthy interior—for instance, by touching your own shit. (Not that you would, of course—or not on purpose.) More important, you must not let your skin become contaminated by anyone else's filthy interior either (except under special circumstances, for which temporary exemptions may be granted). Thus the *apertures* become the most threatening places on the body—the mouth, anus, ears, nostrils, and for women, of course, the vagina—because these apertures are forever vulnerable, inviting penetration and thus contamination. Our apertures make us permeable, but we desire not to be—or only under those special circumstances, like sexual attraction or when in love, and even then the desired permeability is frequently achieved only in tragically defended and self-limiting ways. Besides which, for most of our lives, unfortunately we are *not* in love, meaning that the bodies of others often produce anxious aversion in lieu of desire; disgust is always right around the corner. And who hasn't had the experience of suddenly *turning* that corner, after which things just aren't the same, and those little physical traits that were once endearing suddenly seem . . . really gross. Or obscurely angering. How many marriages could have been saved by separate bathrooms?

These apertures are also deeply related to your sense of self, often laughably precarious or comically armored too. Having a body punctured by so many openings and canals blurs the distinction between inside and outside, self and world. The apertures invariably take on emotional resonance; our relation to them can become psychologically momentous. Your relation to these apertures is also central to the project of forming a personality type, or so Freud thought—an idea that's long since entered general social wisdom, as we routinely perform such diagnoses in everyday social life: She's so "open." He's a real "tightass." "You cunt."

Then we have the embarrassing matter of what emerges from these apertures. Bodily products are socially ranked from the "cleanest" (tears) to the "dirtiest" (shit, vomit). These rankings may reside below consciousness, but they stage-manage our activities and emotions nonetheless. "Clean" body products give rise to empathetic feelings: tears provoke sympathy and are often deployed to that effect, particularly by women; the "dirtier" bodily products provoke avoidance, contempt, and disgust.

If, psychologically speaking, dirt is symbolically linked to what emerges from the body, if our own bodies exude filth at every aperture, then isn't calling something or someone "dirty" essentially a projection? Since what's actually dirty, unfortunately, is . . . you. After all, the main event in the socialization process is toilet training, instilling various degrees of bodily shame in everyone. And if you think you're exempt, some sort of a "free spirit," please take a second to contemplate the possibility of having an "accident" in public—propelled back to that soiled infantile state before the toilet was as securely implanted in your mental landscape, before those distinctions between "clean" and "dirty" were so firmly installed. Now examine your subsequent feelings about yourself, postaccident. Children have to be *taught* not to play with their own shit, and the fact that most of us have indeed renounced this early pleasure is one index of just how effective bodily socialization is. Engaging in such forms of infantile fun in later life is typically regarded as a perversion only a shade less detestable than bestiality or necrophilia. Additionally, our thresholds of disgust about such bodily matters have risen exponentially with sanitation advances, making our bodies even more dirty as civilization marches on. Medieval peasants who shat in public, wiped their snotty noses on their sleeves, and then ate from communal bowls with their hands (before the spread of silverware, hands, knives, and a piece of bread served as eating implements) were far less neurotic about dirt than we moderns. Neurosis is civilization's trade-off for improvements in personal hygiene: we smell better, we have fewer gastric ailments, but we fret about it all far more.

Every society has some kind of sexual division of labor—men do these tasks, women do those—what sort of division it should be is what's under renegotiation in ours. As we know, the female domestic role has been a little contentious over the last three or four decades: the recent history of feminism is, among other things, a protracted argument about who does the cleaning up. Yet the Housework Problem remains a bloody battlefield in contemporary gender relations. The usual explanation for the strife involves the increasing numbers of women in the workforce, since along with it came the affliction of "the second shift," as sociologist Arlie Russell Hochschild designated it, the annoying fact that somehow women—even in couples where the gal outearns the guy or works longer hours—are generally still the ones stuck doing the vast majority of the housework, some 75 percent of it, according to surveys.

Needless to say, being in charge of all the dirt has not made women particularly *jovial*. Especially once second-wave feminism entered the picture, redefining housework as a political issue and demanding wages in recompense (good luck on that) or domestic parity with men (ditto)—in some cases with accompanying contracts enumerating who does what, and how often, and on what days of the week. But even for self-proclaimed nonfeminists, the housework issue has become an oozing domestic sore, particularly once working hours started increasing for everyone. As with most social problems, those at the top of the disposable-income ranks feel the problem less acutely, since other females can be hired to deal with the dirt. (Shifting factors like immigration and unemployment determine who exactly can afford this solution—the "servant problem" traces back to the turn of the twentieth century, when industrial jobs began competing with domestic service for immigrant labor.) Still, even in households featuring two adults working full-time, supervising the cleaning—hiring the help, knowing what needs doing, allocating the tasks, and having the shit fit when they go undone—remains the designated female role.

Are things "improving" on the sexual division of household labor? Reports from the younger generation are mixed. Men raised by feminist mothers will do more cleaning, according to anecdotal reports. But will women let them? This remains unclear. In an unhappy tale related by a twenty-four-year-old woman writing pseudonymously in the recent essay collection *The Bitch in the House,* we hear that younger women too are frequently angry about dirt and housework—even when they're not the ones actually *doing* it. Our author is cohabiting with a boyfriend, there are no kids, and both work long hours. The boyfriend has demonstrated domestic skills and self-sufficiency and is considerate, kind, and attentive. Nevertheless, coming home to a sink full of dirty dishes sends the author into a fuming rage. Not that she's even expected to wash these dishes—at least not by the boyfriend. But there's something about housework she just *feels* more acutely than he does. Spying a pile of dirty dishes in the sink sets her to scorekeeping—"an awful silent process of tallying up and storing away and keeping tabs on what he helped out with and what he did not." He can absorb himself in his after-work hobbies despite the dirty dishes in the kitchen; she can't. Her mind keeps returning to those dishes, like an OCD sufferer, and because they're inescapably on her mind, she finds herself performing more of the housework, and then more of the cooking, despite the boyfriend's offers to do it instead. He offers to cook, he offers to clean, he proposes they go out to eat. Weirdly, his very offers fill her with rage. Predictably, the scorekeeping is followed by . . . more anger. The truth, she finally realizes, is that she *wants* to be angry, though she has no idea why.

More tales from the younger generation: a twenty-eight-year-old professional woman who declares in conversation that cleaning really *isn't* a gender issue anymore, it's just an individual thing now—though she herself is an admitted "clean freak" with deeply held opinions on the relative merits of different name-brand abrasive cleaners (Soft Scrub rules)—also reports that her live-in boyfriend refuses to change the cat litter. Just won't do it..When she had to leave town on a ten-day business trip, she told him he would have to, *please,* just this *once,* change the cat litter while she was gone. She returned on a subzero winter day to find the windows flung wide open and the apartment reeking of cat shit and cat piss. The litter hadn't been changed once; the poor cat was hiding under the bed. But she's also sure that cleaning isn't a gender issue anymore, even if the cleaning roles divide neatly along traditional gender lines. It begins to appear that the younger generation isn't always entirely coherent on the subject of cleaning either.

When it comes to men and housework at the moment, the conventional line on the subject tends to go like this: yes, men now do more around the house than previously (though reportedly often expecting displays of gratitude in return); still, it's the rare man who does anywhere near 50 percent, even with a partner working full-time. As Hochschild reports in *The Second Shift*, while many couples now *claim* to believe in sharing the housework, few do, in actuality, really share the housework in any demonstrably equal way. Instead, many couples create what she calls "modest delusional systems": private mythologies that allow both the male and the female to maintain—contrary to all empirical evidence—that the male does far more than he actually does. For instance the household is divided in "half," with the male responsible for the garage and basement and the female for everything else. This is entirely fascinating—"delusions of housework" as a new national syndrome—but at least it allows couples to avoid showdowns and coexist peacefully.

Though maybe not for long, since, according to Hochschild, men's refusal to really share the housework isn't just the big hurdle for gender equality: the whole future of heterosexual marriage probably hangs in the balance. Hochschild's subjects cite men's creative cleaning-avoidance stratagems as a major cause of marital fractiousness and divorce. Nevertheless, Hochschild herself is opposed to the fallback middle-class solution of hiring household help, even when the couple can afford it; what she wants is for men to *do* their 50 percent of the housework, thus redefining domestic work as not automatically the female's province, and eventually revaluing the whole social enterprise, since activities that men dominate or even merely participate in get more respect.

There are glimmers on the horizon that male and female cleaning proclivities may be in flux—Hochschild says that the less "traditional" the woman, the more "casual" her attitude about the state of the floors and counters is likely to be. But then we come to another troubling wrinkle in the whole sordid saga of dirt and gender, which is that even when men *are* willing to do more housework than in the past, the word around the culture is that they generally manage to do it *badly*. Somehow they just don't sufficiently *care* about dirt. They don't *notice* what needs doing, or what household items need replacing; that the sink is crammed with dishes, and the laundry still in the basket. They're rather indifferent about it all, thus inept.

Possibly men are just outstrategizing women when it comes to playing cleaning chicken: you know, the game where whoever blinks first ends up vacuuming. Some commentators have gone so far as to posit "neurological differences" between men and women to account for women's propensity to care more about cleanliness. Or maybe it's those pesky hormones females got saddled with: women themselves report premenstrual and prepartum cleaning frenzies. Others prefer to blame external villains: patriarchy and social conditioning, along with that other favored culprit, the advertising industry, for marketing a lot of overpriced cleaning products to women and promulgating impossible housekeeping standards while not-so-subtly tying your self-worth to the sheen on your bathroom tile. Mothers have some explaining to do too: women say they feel enslaved to the domestic examples set by previous generations, Stepford Daughters mindlessly emulating Mom's uptight routines while resenting her deeply for them.

All of these excellent explanations leave it completely unclear how women have managed to unlearn traditional femininity sufficiently to run corporations, serve in military combat units in Iraq, argue before the Supreme Court, and adopt a thousand other so-called male behaviors—including stomping all over traditional sexual morality—but somehow can't seem to overthrow the imperative to clean or the propensity to generally *care* more about cleaning than men do.

Feminist godmother Betty Friedan held the sunny view that paying jobs were the solution to the festering female resentment and soul-killing ennui afflicting the full-time housewife. But Friedan also thought women were fundamentally neurotic about housework, observing a little sardonically that housewifery invariably expanded to fill the time allotted for it. Friedan maintained—and this sounds even more incendiary now than when she wrote it—that women with full-time jobs could do the same amount of housework as full-time homemakers in half the time or less, minus the housewife fatigue. And so could men, by the way. Friedan gleefully relates the story of a Minneapolis bachelor-schoolteacher who made the public claim that women who complained about the overburden of housework were just inefficient. When challenged by a local newspaper to prove it, he commandeered a household with four children, ages two to seven, for three days and won his case, outbaking and outcleaning the lady of the house—which she herself later admitted. Friedan also compared two neighbors with identical homes and the same number of children, observing that the one with the full-time job whizzed through the housework so much more efficiently that she still had time for hobbies and reading in the evening, while the full-time housewife was a harried, overworked, angst-ridden mess who never seemed to finish the chores. The message was clear: if a woman's work is never done, it's only because being a full-time housewife-mother is so tedious and unrewarding that women become perversely overinvested in it.

Another feminist pioneer, Simone de Beauvoir, also harbored disdain for females who take a little too well to housewifery. Maniacal housekeepers wage their furious war on dirt, Beauvoir said, "blaming life itself for the rubbish all living growth entails," and if a living being dares to enter the house, she resents it because it just creates more thankless work. Housecleaning obviously makes women a little ridiculous for the soignée Beauvoir. In fact, it becomes a brand of madness verging on perversity: women can't be existentially free because we're too busy fruitlessly exerting petty control over household minutiae. Beauvoir claims that any act *can* be carried out freely—even scouring a stove can be an existential act once the prevailing structures of oppression are dismantled. But she's also clearly horrified by the prospect: scouring lacks magnificence, and women's assignment to the tedious world of maintenance is yet another sorry element in the ongoing indignity of being female.

So here we are, half a century later, and the rancid-dishcloth dilemma still hovers over domestic arrangements like . . . a bad smell. Meanwhile, accusatory debates about working mothers and their household help percolate through women's culture, with various factions lining up to accuse one another of bad faith or bad mothering: *"Why bother having children if you're not going to be there when they come home from school!"*

In recent years, journalist Caitlin Flanagan has been one of the notable finger-pointers. A self-proclaimed antifeminist who writes on domestic issues, Flanagan likes playing the provocateur, most notoriously in a lengthy 2004 *Atlantic* magazine essay with the mildly incendiary title "How Serfdom Saved the Women's Movement." Here she berates professional-class working women—a cohort she likes to tar as "feminists," though perhaps not everyone would agree that simply receiving a paycheck qualifies a gal for such an onerous label—for having coasted to career success on the backs of their exploited housekeepers and nannies, typically lower-class immigrant women whose Social Security taxes their privileged employers refuse to pay. Those feminists: what *elitists*. What *bitches!* The point about Social Security set-asides isn't wrong; it's just that Flanagan's so much more revved up about dressing down ladies-who-work than about the plight of underpaid domestic workers. (As it happens, Flanagan has also written, more than once, about her own feelings of abandonment as a teenager when her mother returned to work, despite the fact that Mom suddenly got a lot less depressed.)

Flanagan says that Hochschild and the other female complainers get it all wrong about men, because these days professional-class men with working wives *are* willing to roll up their shirtsleeves and pitch in. The problem, says Flanagan, is that women simply have *higher standards* about how the housework should be done than men do, thus guaranteeing that either women will end up doing the majority of it themselves, or in a perpetually foul mood about the cruddy countertops.

> [Men] can be cajoled into doing all sorts of household tasks, but they will not do them the way a woman would. They will bathe the children, but they will not straighten the bath mat and wring out the washcloths . . . They will in other words, do what men have always done: reduce a job to its essentials and utterly ignore the fillips and niceties that women tend to regard as equally essential.

Flanagan's solution? She herself employs a brigade of household help: both a nanny *and* a maid; she's also a proud stay-at-home mom. (She likes to refer to her writing career as "a hobby.") Flanagan leads rather a charmed life:

> I have never once argued with my husband about which of us was going to change the sheets of the marriage bed, but then—to my certain knowledge—neither one of us ever has changed the sheets. Or scrubbed the bathtubs, or dusted the cobwebs off the top of the living room bookcase, or used the special mop and the special noncorrosive cleanser on the hardwood floors. Two years ago our little boys got stomach flu, one right after the other, and there were ever so many loads of wash to do, but we did not do them. The nanny did.

If Flanagan's point is that men don't care enough about cleaning to do it to women's satisfaction, does the converse argument hold true too: Do women care a smidgen *too* much for cleaning? Is there something about cleanliness that peculiarly . . . *gratifies* some element of the feminine psyche?

It's not exactly news that the bourgeois female role centers on caring about how things look: what theme is more front and center in traditional femininity than appearance anxiety, in all its facets. Women frequently take the appearance of the household as a commentary on themselves: appearance anxiety can attach equally to your domicile or your outfit. (Children don't escape scrutiny here either, little mini-me's that they are. The pursuit of upper-middle-class domestic perfection now encompasses not just homes but also childrearing, given the style of obsessive, labor-intensive parenting now in fashion in the United States, at least in the upper demographics.*)

In journalist Peggy Orenstein's *Flux,* an account of changing female roles and women's conflicts about them, we encounter Jill, a suburban Minneapolis insurance-company VP and mother of three, who's commandeered her hapless husband and daugh-

---

*A few childrearing heretics have recently dared to point out that kids aren't particularly better off for all this overattention and chauffeuring and the limitless expressions of parental narcissism. If children have replaced men as objects of female romantic fantasy (men having proven washouts once too often on the fantasy front), will children fare any better at fulfilling female yearnings? Be less disappointing as romantic objects? You have to wonder what industrial-strength varieties of neurosis will soon be appearing in this generation of overparented children as they near adulthood.

ters into a "major housecleaning" in preparation for Orenstein's casual visit. Jill explains: "I feel like if my house is messy or my kids don't have clean clothes, people are going to judge me." Her husband somehow lacks this predisposition. Hochschild too noted that the working women she interviewed often began the interviews by apologizing for the state of the house: as if messiness reflected something about them personally, as if their self-esteem were hanging in the balance. Women who thought of themselves as more progressive—those committed to sharing the housework with husbands—*tried* harder not to care how the house looked "and proudly told me about things they'd let go of or forgotten to do," Hochschild relates, but this usually took some effort. "On the whole, women cared more about how the house looked than men did. When they didn't care, they struggled harder against their upbringing and exerted more emotional effort to stop caring about the house."

What none of these accounts manage to tell us is *why*, despite the numerous transformations in the female role, this deranged self-identification of women with cleaning has so much psychological staying power, or how it is that women have managed to overthrow the shackles of *chastity*—to cite another rather significant vestige of traditional femininity—more easily than bondage to the vacuum cleaner.

A clue arrives from an unlikely source, a September 2002 *O, The Oprah Magazine* article titled "Are You *TOO* Clean?" Mulling over the difficulties of choosing the right facial cleanser for your particular skin type, the author quotes a spokeswoman for

Shiseido Prestige Brands about a new product line: "The women we observe in focus groups scrub their faces as if they're scrubbing their kitchen counters, using brisk, back-and-forth motions and excessive friction." Ouch. But exactly what form of dirtiness is being so energetically attacked by these brisk lady scrubbers, and will a brutal enough scrubbing finally get it clean? Another clue with similar connotations comes from former professional housekeeper Louise Rafkin, who writes in *Other People's Dirt,* an offbeat memoir about her adventures in sanitation, "Cleaning helps me deal with the feelings in my body."

Perhaps the shape of the problem begins to come into focus: the household and the body stand in for each other at some not entirely conscious level. But here's the complication: Wouldn't scrubbing away at unwelcome feelings also serve the dual purpose of confirming them? Can you scrub away an existential condition?

If the Housework Problem plunges us into certain "deeper issues" at the core of femininity, one of those deeper issues, all too clearly, is sex. Dirt and sex: always such a fun couple, strolling hand in hand through history. In our time, they seem to pop up rather frequently in the voluminous self-help literature devoted to the pitfalls of modern marriage and coupledom, particularly in the context of that most painful marital dilemma of our day: sexual anesthesia. Yes, sorry to say, lack of sexual desire is apparently an alarmingly common affliction among the heterosexual couples of our nation. The situation is this: boy meets girl, they fall in love, marry, go at it like lust-crazed monkeys for a few years, then for some strange reason . . . just stop wanting to have sex with each other. Or worse, one person stops wanting to have sex, and the other is very peevish about it. Tune into a daytime talk show, visit a bookstore, peruse *New Yorker* cartoons, and you will learn that "sexless marriages are an undeniable epidemic," as one prominent advice guru, the folksy yet unctuous Dr. Phil, phrases it. And the most prevalent explanation for marital sexlessness, say the experts, is the inherent desire-killing properties for women of doing far more than their fair share of the housework, then bunking down with an oblivious male partner who just "doesn't notice" the dust balls rolling across the living room floor like tumbleweeds, manages to overlook the diminishing state of the toilet-paper supply, and thinks that greasy, food-encrusted dishes can be left until tomorrow. Who could get aroused in such a situation?

But help is on the way. In the massively best-selling book *Men Are from Mars, Women Are from Venus*—some fourteen million copies purchased since 1992, translated into forty languages— John Gray offers men "101 Ways to Score Points with a Woman." A full twenty-one of those points involve performing household chores: washing the dishes, making the bed, offering to pick up items at the market, and so on. "Doing chores is one of the best forms of foreplay," counsels Gray; shirking housework is a surefire way for men to get less sex. Hard-up husbands of the world,

take note: "When she feels responsible for everything, her ability to enjoy sex is diminished." If men could simply *notice* the
household minutiae that women notice, they'd see a lot more
action between the sheets.

And if women noticed these details *less,* would our sex lives
perk up too? Sadly, not noticing does not appear to be an option
for females in these accounts. Thus we find Jennifer Worick,
author of *How to Live with a Man . . . and Love It!,* counseling
women to "make it easy for your man to keep things tidy" by
keeping a laundry hamper in the corner of the bedroom so you
won't be distracted during lovemaking by an unsightly heap of
dirty clothes on the floor. As one reviewer observed tartly, "Beyond the simple assumption that men are dirty lies a fear of sexual intimacy so fragile that dirty laundry would disrupt it." Joan
Didion leveled a similar charge in a scathing 1972 essay on the
women's movement, diagnosing in women's complaints about
men's dirty-mindedness an aversion "to adult sexual life itself:
how much cleaner to stay forever children." (Women who complain about things like construction workers whistling at them
are acting like "wounded birds," Didion delicately snorted.)

But what exactly is it about dirt that keeps impeding sexual
harmony between men and women? And why the constant
accusation mode: one sex somehow more *polluted* than the
other; one sex always offending or sullying or reprimanding the
other? (Though occasionally the charge is that someone isn't
dirty *enough:* the accusation of sexual prudishness, usually aimed
at a female, though once in a while at an undersexed man.) Clas-

sicist and poet Anne Carson summarizes the dilemma rather elegantly in an essay on the theme of women and dirt in antiquity: "As members of human society, perhaps the most difficult task we face daily is that of touching one another—whether the touch is physical, moral, emotional, or imaginary. Contact is crisis."

Note that the dirt-sex dilemma hasn't only played out in the nation's kitchens and bathrooms, it's left its mark on history as well, and nowhere more conspicuously than in the female social-purity movement of the mid- to late nineteenth century. The "movement" was actually hundreds of separate organizations and campaigns, with rousing names like the National Vigilance Association and the Moral Reform Union, variously devoted to anti-vice agitation and temperance campaigns, rallying against gambling, prostitution, and general male sexual loucheness. All this first took off in England and the United States, eventually spawning international organizations and world congresses aimed at cleaning up male behavior everywhere. Themes of public hygiene and sanitary reform were tied to morality campaigns, with women undertaking to purify society on *all* levels, public and private, through legislation, street-corner proselytizing, or whatever it took.

Basically, the social-purity crowd wanted men to just keep it zipped. While first-wave feminists were out campaigning for the vote and legal rights, and female socialists were aligning with men in the nascent labor movement, social-purity aims were actually more radical: to revamp the idea that male sexuality was any sort of biological imperative and promote self-control instead, letting sexually beleaguered females off the hook and improving all of society in the process. In effect, it was a fight over the sexual double standard, though not, unfortunately, in the name of more sexual freedom for women (this was left to a handful of plucky free-love proponents)—the plan was that men too should have to adhere to the conduct required of sexually corseted females. Inspiring guilt about dirty male sexual urges was one important tactic; surprisingly, this caught on with more than a few men, who went on to form male chastity leagues of their own, devoted to battling pernicious literature and dirty postcards and eliminating the scourge of masturbation. One male group, the Alliance of Honor, actually grew to over 100,000 members—spin-offs included the Boy Scouts and the Salvation Army, both of which carry on their good works to this day.

Politically, a consequential new line of thinking was emerging: the idea that there simply wasn't a unity of interests between men and women when it came to sex. Additionally, women were morally superior to men, because female sexuality was primarily mental, not physical; male sexuality was associated with dirtiness in need of a good scrubbing and women were the moral force uniquely equipped for the job. The question is how *women,* who not so long before—up until the eighteenth century even—were regarded as the bawdier sex, suddenly became so sanitary and full of rectitude, the nation's new moral watchdogs? Piety and virtue had once been regarded as human qualities, not womanly ones. Yes, the feminization of virtue really was the nineteenth century's booby prize to women—and many thanks to the social-purity set for the lasting legacy of sexless maternal femininity and female moral self-righteousness.

In retrospect it make sense that with the rise of industrialization in the nineteenth century, a compensatory cult of domesticity took hold. The home became a sanctified realm removed from the tawdriness of the marketplace, and it was the new sentimentality about the home that gave women the platform to assert a new public authority as guardians of national purity. When Frances Willard, founder of the Woman's Christian Temperance Union, pronounced that her goal was "to make the whole world houselike," she was floating a new political ideology: that the strength of the nation was directly connected to the strength of the nation's households. The problem with dividing the world into these increasingly separate male and female domains was that it wasn't just paid work that was assigned to the male sphere, it was sexuality as well. On their side of the divide, men got sexual passion; women got cleanup duty. Once again, thanks. On the other hand, there were certain compensations in desexualization: birthrates dropped dramatically throughout the nineteenth century; women were at least managing to wrest more autonomy over their bodies out of the new equation.

Still, embarking on the social cleanup mission as a route to empowerment also had clear drawbacks: if spotless homes were the foundation of a properly run society, whose job was it to keep them spotless? Women were now increasingly expected to invest psyches and beings in the cleanliness program, and all the more so toward the end of the century, as Pasteur's theories on bacteria gained hold, and the war on household dust and microscopic pathogens seized the public imagination, replacing earlier theories about miasmas and the disease-inducing properties of bad smells. The germ theory of disease really sealed women's fate: even more vigilant disinfecting and sanitizing were demanded to chase down the invisible enemy, and as with all unseen threats, zealotry is pretty much a given. But sanitation reform was also the fast track to female empowerment— recall Florence Nightingale, that great sanitizer, and one of the most influential women of the nineteenth century.

No one here's objecting to sanitation, quite the contrary. Though let's keep in mind that sanitation was an upper-class luxury that only gradually filtered down the social hierarchy, along with innovations like piped water and proper sewers— none of which impeded the moralizing dimension of cleanliness, which had already been in play for a while. The Reverend John Wesley's keen insight that "Cleanliness is, indeed, next to godliness" dates from 1788, though the sentiment certainly predates him. Despite the moral flap, cleanliness and purity have never really been identical: dung was an important element in ancient purity rituals; and the water in a mikvah—the Orthodox Jewish ritual bath—isn't always quite as clean as you might hope. (In a few embarrassing instances local health departments have intervened, performing overly revealing tests on the bacteria count in the purifying waters.) None of which has ever stopped beliefs about contagion and pollution from being linked to ideas about morality, and all the more intensely as civilization progresses, and with all the welcome advances in sanitation technology. Consider the psychological effects of the flush toilet alone—goodbye to chamber pots, all your bodily wastes thankfully whisked from sight, now only a vague memory—allowing the ever-pertinent question "You think your shit doesn't stink?" to enter the social lexicon. Consider too, the new varieties of class contempt directed at the unwashed: if cleanliness is virtuous and the distribution of cleaning advances invariably begins with the moneyed, obviously rich and poor deserve their respective fates. After all, who's cleaner?

The connection of cleanliness with virtue is one of humankind's most sustaining lies. And what a self-congratulatory story it is—at least if you think you fall on the right side of the dirt-virtue equation, that is. The deleterious effects on the female psyche have yet to be undone.

As the twentieth century rolled around, the growth of commercial culture and newfangled technologies like electricity and indoor plumbing were fast revamping the housewife role.

Cleanliness standards before running water had been sketchy at best for domiciles *and* bodies, despite all the sanitizing verbiage. Now, with expectations about cleanliness rising, so was anxiety about it—and rising across the industrialized world, though with different national inflections. (Scandinavian countries took to cleaning morality with zeal; southern Europe a little less so.) Hygiene standards and disgust thresholds also rocketed up as cleanliness technologies advanced: concepts of purity and contamination may be universal, but cleaning regimes themselves are socially specific. Consider that prior to manufactured clothing made of lightweight materials like cotton, outer clothes were washed rarely (they were aired or brushed); even underclothes, when worn, weren't often changed or laundered—an appealing thought for the contemporary BO-phobic sensibility. In the earlier part of the nineteenth century, soap was scarce (mass-produced only after 1875) and bathing itself was controversial: some authorities insisted that it promoted disease, though given the difficulty of hauling and heating water, it was a rare event for most of the population anyway. In other words, people basically reeked, though the rich may have reeked a little less.

Needless to say, housewives and their psyches were at the center of all these advances. With new labor-saving devices, plus all the new packaged goods and ready-made consumer items, maintaining the appearance of the household began overtaking household production as the new female role. ("Labor-saving" may be a misnomer: historians of housework disagree about whether the modern innovations actually increased or de-

creased the amount of labor required to maintain a household.)
The fledgling captains of industry quickly figured out that there
were big profits to be extracted from middle-class women who
identified their self-worth with cleanliness; thus an ascendant
consumer culture set about bludgeoning housewives with a
steady stream of overanxious cleaning advice dedicated to abol-
ishing unseen dirt and fostering emotional identifications with
cleaning brands. The advertising industry was, after all, more or
less founded on the marketing of soap, and women were the
population it was marketed to, in pitches brilliantly capitalizing
on female cleansing and beautifying aspirations. Note that advertising was also one of the new professions most hospitable to
hiring women, grasping early on that women are the ones who
know best how to undermine other women (as every woman
knows somewhere deep within her being, underneath the gooey
sisters-stick-together stuff). By 1920, pioneering female-authored
ads plastered the country, targeting uniquely female forms of
anxious dirtiness like "conspicuous nose pores." What do men
know about nose pores? This was female-on-female emotional
sabotage.

With the twentieth-century female consumer shouldering
aside the nineteenth century's moral beacon, the female role
was becoming more socially trivial. The phrase "just a housewife" entered the vocabulary by the 1920s. As the social worth
of housework decreased, displeasure about being the one stuck
doing it escalated. The image of the bored housewife was becoming a national stereotype. Meanwhile, the number of fe-

male college graduates was on the rise: women were being educated to do something more in the world than change diapers and mop floors, but found themselves doing exactly that once married. Friedan's 1963 *Feminine Mystique* cataloged the epidemic of desperation and seething resentment in highly educated women leading extremely privileged lives, which felt to them like stultifying domestic cages. At her darkest, Friedan reads like a Fellini of the suburbs: the mise-en-scène is grotesque, but with unexpectedly comedic twists. One of her sources, a local doctor, captures the prevailing mood like this: "You'd be surprised at the number of those happy suburban wives who simply go berserk one night and run shrieking through the street without any clothes on."

Along came second-wave feminism, with Friedan as the founding spirit of a movement soon to replay most of the same splits that had divided the first-wave activists in the previous century. Liberal feminists focused on rights-based themes like equal pay, fighting discrimination, and reproductive freedom, while radical feminists seized on the old social-purity motifs: namely, the preoccupation with men's *dirtiness*, from their failure to share the housework to their sexual dirtiness.* There were distressing new scourges to combat: not germs, but "the objectification of women" ("dirty-mindedness"), the pornography plague ("filth"), even sex jokes at work came in for sanita-

---

*What were deemed the "radical" factions in 1970s feminism often ended up espousing the most conservative positions on sexual politics.

tion. For some reason, female reformism just keeps returning to the theme of *dirt;* male cleansing of one sort or another is the fundamental demand.

Of course, assigning all the dirtiness in the world to men does have the advantage of settling the age-old question "Which sex is the dirtiest?" *Not women! Not us!* But is the role of keeping things clean forever to be the female plight? Is *this* the price of "empowerment": women are supposed to spend the rest of eternity in the absurd Sisyphus-like task of ridding the world of dirt?

If the body itself is the real culprit when it comes to dirt, and if bodily apertures are the subtext of all the anxiety, well, women *are* the sex encumbered by one too many of them, as Dr. Kubie kindly points out in "The Fantasy of Dirt": "the one aperture whose presence makes the most urgent protest." And isn't it just a woman's stupid luck that it's an aperture that also exudes sticky gloppy streams of blood on a monthly basis. yes, it's a *very* dirty aperture. In contamination studies, the vagina is shown to have high "contamination sensitivity"—construed by those possessing one as a highly vulnerable bodily point, far more so than the mouth, for instance, which actually has to bear much more traffic in and out, no matter how great your sex life, or how stringent your current diet. Vaginas also have high contamination *potency:* objects that come in contact with a vagina are seen by most as irrevocably contaminated. (The ear is the most benign aperture, in both respects.)

Recall the unhappy fact that throughout history there's been the universal conviction that women are somehow dirtier than men. The male body is regarded, or is symbolically, as cleaner than the female body, despite the conscious popular attitude (at least since the nineteenth century) that men are the dirty sex. Possibly it's that outjutting parts of the body, like a penis, are regarded as somehow cleaner than holes and cavities: softness, wetness, and sliminess are usually felt to be dirtier than hardness and dryness. If it's a rock versus a swamp, the rock wins this game, unfair as it may be to the swamp. In fact, the rock-swamp contest is a good metaphor for the problem under discussion: the problem of the female body.

Will social progress manage to erase the millennial history of bodily aversions and projections between the sexes? History would indicate not. At least not so far, since cultures worldwide have believed that women are somehow *polluting,* that female bodies, especially when menstruating, are dangerous to men's health and often to other entities, like crops and livestock, too. All bodily secretions are construed as dirty (tears are the exception), but menstrual fluids are even dirtier than the rest, possibly even lethal. The vagina is frequently associated with rot and decay, a gateway through which evil enters the world. In fact, the entire female body is frequently seen as a source of dangerous contagion, subject to bizarre taboos and superstitions, many of which persist into the present. Though let's not forget to look at the upside: the abiding belief in female destructiveness has inspired some of the world's most enduring art and literature.

Throughout the generations, men—often aided and abetted by women themselves, it must be said—have contrived an array of weird decontamination rituals to shield themselves from female poisons: isolating themselves from women (or women from them), having sex at their own peril, sometimes preferring to remain bachelors rather than risk contact with the female vagina, or venturing near one only when protected by talismans or other defensive protocols. In some cultures, menstruating women can't prepare or serve food, aren't supposed to go into the forest because they would jinx it, and are enjoined from touching crucial items like sleeping blankets or hunting bows. (Paradoxically, other practices idealizing women and glorifying femininity often appear in tandem with contamination fears.) No doubt men shrink from female bodies out of their own sexual desires and vulnerabilities, from terror about fertility and procreation—a jumble of polarized emotions that are as unstable as they are irresolvable, says anthropologist David Gilmore in a fascinating cross-cultural study of misogyny. As Gilmore puts it: "It is no exaggeration to say that the greatest obsession in history is that of man with woman's body."

Virtually all major religions abominate the female body in some fashion, regarding it as tainted and impure, also abhorring those unseemly monthly discharges. Rules governing marital relations among Orthodox Jews dictate that husbands and wives forgo sex from the beginning of the wife's menstrual period until seven days after it ends, resuming only after she's had a mikvah, or ritual purifying bath; before that, she's considered unclean. The Koran imposes similar restrictions. These are not antiquated beliefs. In 2005, the *New York Times* reported that a new mikvah was opening in a posh Upper East Side neighborhood in Manhattan, in a renovated town house with mahogany doors and marble tiling; in Easthampton, New York, another tony enclave, a group of investors was constructing a new mikvah in a renovated pool house. The target audience: upper-middle-class career women.

Secular culture has its menstrual superstitions too: a 1981 report by the Tampax company found that half of the one thousand Americans surveyed believed women shouldn't have intercourse when menstruating. And we have our secular purity rites: the next time you watch a tampon or sanitary-napkin commercial on TV, note the omnipresent white-on-white motif of the backdrops and wardrobes. Obviously, menstrual mishaps are not without their elements of shame even in our sexually progressive times: no matter what kind of an enlightened chick you are, discovering you've been walking around all day with a big red stain on the back of your skirt is an occasion for extended self-mortification. But even minus visible stains, the contamination effect is present. In 2002, researchers studying how menstruation shaped attitudes toward women found that when a participant in the study "inadvertently" dropped a tampon from her handbag, the research subjects, male and female college students, sat farther away from her than when a neutral item like a hair clip was dropped. In contamination studies, the majority (69 percent) of subjects, both men and women, were unwilling to put a new, unused, and previously wrapped tampon in their mouth; 3 percent wouldn't even touch it.

Psychiatrist Kubie tells of female patients encumbered by the feeling that they can never get clean and struggling with a constant compulsion to *prove* their cleanliness, shamed by this persistent sense of inner dirtiness. (Consider joining a social-purity movement!) More recently, in studies of obsessive cleaning and washing compulsions, psychologists have found that women report more contamination obsessions than men do, scoring higher in OCD-related fears and engaging in more "ritualistic neutralizing behaviors." Which is to say, *washing and cleaning*.

Aren't such "ritualistic neutralizing behaviors" actually just somewhat exaggerated versions of what we regard as normal femininity? To date, a certain neurotic bodily self-relation does remain the female inheritance, sad to say. Kubie calls women's incessant discontent with their bodies—the endless efforts to alter its shape and features—"compulsive cosmetic compensations." By "compensation," he means a solution to the one-too-many-apertures problem. But "compulsive"? How could anyone think there's something *compulsive* about the numerous time-consuming beautifying procedures and ablutions that most of us females ritually perform before leaving the house and presenting our fatally flawed, often secretly bleeding bodies for public inspection—even those of us armed to the teeth with feminist theory or Madonnaesque postmodern irony about femininity? Kubie's point seems to be that even the most everyday "normal" feminine rituals are constructed along the lines of defense mechanisms—defenses against unconscious feelings of dirtiness; the endless beautifying a mechanism to counter that felt sense of ugliness, by sheer cosmetic force.

A late-breaking development on the cosmetic compensation front: the new focus on grooming and fashioning—what else?— the *vagina* and its surrounding environs. Pubic hair now needs regular waxing for the fashion-conscious babe: screechingly painful, yes, but what's a hairy girl to do? "Designer vaginas" are the new trend in cosmetic surgery: you may want to alter the vaginal lips, reduce or plump up the labia with fat removal or injections, perhaps make the whole business more symmetrical. You can liposuction the pubic area for a more youthful look, or tighten the vagina itself—"vaginal rejuvenation"—for that youthful feel. Some ladies are even opting to restore their hymens. A Chicago sex therapist who conducted a national survey on the effect of women's "genital self-image on sexual function" reports that most women "walk around with a feeling of anxiety about their genitals."

None of which is such great news for the cause of female emancipation. Unconscious filth convictions and the ritual by-product compensations they entail would tend to impinge on the quest for autonomy and freedom, the primary existential dilemma for all of us shackled humans, but a far worse dilemma for the female of the species, who always seems to get plunked with the hard end of the social-repression stick. Along with most of the housework, of course.

Freud thought he knew why women are so susceptible to housecleaning zealotry. Along Kubie's line, it's because of that perceived inner stain. Vaginas are regarded by the world as dirty, and that sense of dirtiness is internalized, with any conscious acknowledgment of those feelings vigorously resisted and defended against—but the defense is a measure of the depth of the injury. Hence all that free-floating female anger—because the whole situation really *is* absurd. (And by the way, why there haven't been more female absurdists is the great cultural mystery—where's *our* Beckett, *our* Ionesco?) Hence, Freud suggests, all the female self-righteousness and moralizing about cleaning standards, and the close attention paid to every facet of dirt, both physical and social: cleaning is never exactly a neutral activity to those assigned a female anatomy. In other words, if women are situated in the world as contaminated, staking out a social role as a cleansing force makes a certain dismal, convoluted sense.

Of course, humans without vaginas aren't immune from genital anxieties either: men too have their "issues." But somehow it's less controversial to propose that men deal with them by overcompensating elsewhere—with their big cigars, and big cars, and pushy behavior—than to voice similar speculations about a woman. Namely, that she might deal with her private anxieties by overcompensating elsewhere too, say in cleaning or grooming behaviors. This proves to be a touchy subject: try raising it and fur will fly, you'll likely be charged with misogyny, or accusations of "biological determinism" will be hurled, as happens with Freud so much of the time, poor guy—so frequently misconstrued as prescribing what he was just trying to describe. (If at times awkwardly.) Unfortunately, what he was attempting to describe—the tangled relationship between anatomy and the psyche—isn't entirely cheery news. Still, he didn't invent the situation. If there's a culprit, it wasn't Freud, it's the human symbolic imagination, an archaic thing, which isn't fully in sync with external realities like social progress. Maybe one day it will catch up.

But you do have to wonder: If women didn't menstruate, would more of us find dirty jokes funnier? Would the cleaning imperative have taken hold a little less successfully, and be abandoned with a little more alacrity? If women didn't have vaginas, would we take fewer bubble baths, be less susceptible to the newest miracle cleaning product's marketing campaign, let up on the cleaning standards (for those prone to occupying the household enforcer role), and *simply not do* more than 50 percent of the housework?

In the meantime, women remain caught between the regimes of modern femininity and the moral high grounding of feminist reformism. And those "standards," of course. Cleaning house, cleaning up society, cleaning up sex, scrubbing away at those

unsightly nose pores: housekeeping of one sort or another remains the female plight. Take an assigned social role—bourgeois
housewife—add the time-honored symbolic baggage of female
anatomy, and voilà, what you have is a large psychological road-
block. Deploying the cleanup imperative to turn the tables on
men does have its satisfactions—though, of course, it also sinks
everyone even deeper into the mire of mutual projection. And
even when women manage to win a round in this match, it's not
so clear that being the cleanest sex is actually the path to anyone's great liberation.

4

VULNERABILITY

If you're a chick, you're sitting on some pretty valuable real estate. Is any other human body cavity quite so laden with symbolic value, not to mention actual monetary worth, particularly for exclusive access? Fathers once traded their virgin daughters for bride payments; nonvirgins were handed over at reduced rates. Even today, play your cards right and a vagina can mean all sorts of social rewards. Just about everywhere on earth, right of entry to the revered female cooze (pootietang, quiff, tunnel of love—what poetry this small furry thing has inspired) can still command wads of cash or cash equivalents, even for non-professionals. Pricey dinners, diamond rings (the exact entry fee is usually negotiable)—in what other system of exchange can you trade exclusive access to an orifice for a suburban split-level and a lifetime of monetary support? Not such a bad deal, considering the backbreaking and alienated things a lot of people end up doing for money.

On the other hand, a vagina is also an extremely *costly* attribute to lug around and makes a woman forever vulnerable—just walking down the street is like wearing a Rolex at a burglars' convention. Or it is pending the happy day when rape is finally eliminated; until then, protecting that prized portal is virtually the bedrock of female experience, leading to timidity, impeded mobility—even basic bodily comportment is affected: you don't see a lot of women sitting with their knees three feet apart, taking up two subway seats, do you? Yes, custodianship of a vagina really *is* the female Achilles' heel, and not just because both are prone to fungal infections (a minor but thoroughly annoying aspect of the vaginal ecosystem). Please be assured that no one here wants to reduce women to a body part—let's leave that to the carloads of adolescent boys yelling endearments like *"Hey, cunt!"* out the window at passing females, and always so gratifying to be reminded that you do indeed have a vagina while you're lugging groceries home or waiting for the bus, in case you'd momentarily forgotten.

Vaginas are assigned so much social worth in the overall somatic schema—but perhaps they're overpriced? After all, no other orifice commands quite so much investment, not just monetary but psychological, literary, mythological . . . No doubt there's always been something a little uncanny about the vagina to begin with: things go in (penises), other things come out (babies—the miracle of human life, if you want to get misty about it). Still, it's not really evident that vagina overpricing ultimately works to female advantage, despite the occasional fringe benefits. For one thing, overvalued things so often provoke that mischievous human urge to demote them: as we know, vaginas aren't only revered, they're also continually denigrated (along with those who possess one, of course). But as indicated, the big problem with these high-value vaginas is that the more they're overpriced, the more theft-prone they become; thus constant vigilance is required to keep out marauders and trespassers, those who would pluck your trophy, steal your jewel, with feigned promises and sweet talk or sometimes even force. Indeed, rape has often been construed as a form of property crime: in the early days the theft was from a father or husband (and remains a violation of family honor in many places); in modern settings, the theft is from the victim herself, robbed of her bodily autonomy, her consent, her civil rights—to some minds, stripped of her very *self.* Vagina overvaluation is such that an inviolate vagina can be construed as worth more than life itself; criminologists studying fear of crime report that the prospect of being raped is seen by a majority of women as worse than being murdered. Needless to say, the idea that you could be minding your own business just walking down the street and someone would simply *decide to put his penis in you* does take some getting used to—and that's pretty much the female situation right there: women have been forced to become accustomed to this bizarre idea, because women got blessed with those wonderfully valuable vaginas but not necessarily with the body strength to defend them, should it prove necessary.

Feminists writing on the subject—Susan Brownmiller's important 1975 *Against Our Will: Men, Women, and Rape,* among others—have generally seen rape as a domination tactic deployed against women as a class, keeping the female population reflexively submissive. (Or at least in a state of perpetual low-level trepidation: a fortyish, recently separated teacher about to try online dating for the first time frets about having men back to her apartment: "What about—you know—the R-word?")

Men rape because they have the anatomical equipment to accomplish the act: once they discovered that they could rape, they happily proceeded to and haven't let up, in Brownmiller's account. Women are not only inherently rapeable; unfortunately, we have no comparable equipment with which to retaliate; men can thus exploit female fear for political and social advantage. Rape is one of culture's ways of *feminizing* women, says Brownmiller, less an aberration than a model of overall relations between the sexes. For the wave of antipornography activists who followed the rape activists, the use of force was also standard operating procedure in male-female sexual transactions. "Pornography is the theory, rape is the practice," as Robin Morgan famously put it, and though the rhetoric has cooled down a bit since those giddy early movement days, the slippery-slope model prevails; there's often still a taint of female *victimization* left hovering around the whole heterosexual scenario.

Also a whiff of female self-delusion? Feminist Catharine MacKinnon declared that any kind of meaningful consent is impossible for women under patriarchy, even when those involved think they're voluntary participants—you may say "Yes," but what you really mean is "I'm your puppet, use me for your pleasure." Of course, not everyone went along with this premise: so-called pro-sex and anti-antiporn feminists scoffed at the MacKinnon line, which they saw as perversely disempowering; they started dissenting journals and held conferences with provocative titles like "Pleasure and Danger" and peddled pro-woman porn. But to those who'd dismiss all this as your grandma's feminism or last century's arguments: look around.

MacKinnon-style thinking not only cut a pretty deep swath through the culture, it's now the party line in virtually any institutional setting. Consider the general state of high alert these days about sexual relations between anyone with different levels of institutional power. Once power was an established aphrodisiac, it was hot; now it's de facto abuse or harassment.

This *was* MacKinnon's basic premise, and it's since wended its way into public policy, workplace mores, and campus regulations across the country. Not to mention national politics: recall the Clinton impeachment, which managed to occupy the nation's attention for a while and alter the political calculation in untold ways. MacKinnon herself exulted, "When Paula Jones sued Bill Clinton, male dominance quaked." Despite the MacKinnon victory boogie, it's not clear that any women other than settlement beneficiary Jones saw much benefit from that lawsuit; in fact, probably the reverse. The whole premise that a single sexual advance causes traumatic (though highly lucrative) injury flourished less because male dominance was teetering than because it reinforced the woman-as-delicate-flower tendencies already present in the culture and fed into a revival of sexual conservatism, abetted by misguided strange-bedfellow alliances between radical feminists and political conservatives, including the Christian right.*

---

*Not only by MacKinnon: when her sidekick, radical feminist Andrea Dworkin died in 2005, leading American conservatives published encomiums to her. A feminist always ready to sabotage feminism for the larger cause, Dworkin had long befriended figures on the cultural and political right, pegging them as her allies against porn and prostitution. More on Dworkin to follow.

What's the advantage to women in any of this? There's no doubt that wallowing in victimhood can sometimes be perversely gratifying: you get to feel so *virtuous*, so Little Red Riding Hood pursued by the Big Bad Wolf. But what does it mean to find the most fluttering varieties of femininity lodged at the epicenter of the most programmatic variety of radical feminism? Or possibly even propelling it?

Of course, we find the same fluttery tendencies at the epicenter of the nation's self-help aisles at the moment as well, where the propensity for female victimization in the emotional and romantic spheres moves a lot of product. What's a little depressing, in both feminism *and* commercial women's culture, is the sense of a certain inevitability that women will be used and wounded by men. Or so one infers from the premises of books like *The Script: The 100% Absolutely Predictable Things Men Do When They Cheat*, coauthored by two rather aggrieved divorced ladies. Whether or not you agreed with it, MacKinnon at least had a political analysis of female injury. Here a trickle-down MacKinnonite logic still drives the story but the politics have withered away, replaced by sheer complaint. The villains aren't rapists and pornographers—well, not *literally*—now they're adulterers, which isn't so far off in this telling. (Bill Clinton serves as the model male, and no punishment would be adequate.) Men are revealed as abusive manipulators and narcissists who care only for their own selfish gratification; women are the blindsided victims, their sole flaw having been too trusting. Did you know that *every* cheating husband exhibits *exactly* the same signs when he cheats? Or that the majority of such guys turn out to be such emotional sadists that they will, for example, have divorce papers served on you at your birthday-party dinner in front of twenty-five guests, then announce, "I'm divorcing you, you bitch" as you blow out the candles on your birthday cake? Carry this book with you at all times: like a can of Mace for the married woman. Especially if you've put on a little weight lately. If your husband buys you an unexpected expensive present, don't be fooled: it's just part of the Script. If he suggests that you take a weekend trip to a spa with your girlfriends, call a lawyer immediately. (The fact is that the majority of divorces are sought by women according to marriage historian Stephanie Coontz, but don't tell the Script authors.)

The tendrils of the sex-as-victimhood concept have now spread far beyond the original purview: the injured parties don't even have to be female anymore. Certainly, feeling injured is a social motif not restricted to the realm of gender—consider the daily parade of loquacious victims and plaintiffs on daytime talk shows and courtroom television, preening for the cameras and flashing their bruises, metaphorical or otherwise. But sexual injury in particular has become the paradigmatic trauma of our time, with the concept now so elastic that everyone can get in on the action, especially since, as MacKinnon instructed, Yes doesn't necessarily have to mean consent. Once a teenage boy was considered rather *lucky* should a kindly older woman take him under her wing, sexually speaking; now he's regarded as a victim of sexual abuse, certain to face a lifetime of post-traumatic stress, and the lusty if ill-advised math teacher or fountain-of-youth-seeking neighbor gets hauled up on statutory rape charges. Another triumph for the forces of sexual protectionism—though ironic that the protectionist momentum ends up throwing women in the slammer for doing what just a few generations earlier playwrights and authors extolled as a social service. Some of us were actually *assigned* to read *Tea and Sympathy* in high school drama classes back in the dark ages—that is, before its denouement would have been considered an act of juvenile sex exploitation. ("When you speak of this in future years—and you will—be kind," says the housemaster's wife as she seduces the gawky, possibly gay college student in a kindly, even therapeutic gesture. In the updated ending, she's led away in handcuffs.)

Make no mistake: it's absolutely the case that feminist political action against rape has had hugely transformative social benefits for women, overhauling the way the criminal justice system treats rape victims. Corroborating evidence standards have changed; rape shield laws prevent the victim's sexual history from being used to humiliate her at trial; and most states now have limits on exemptions for marital rape. Date rape has been politicized; more women have learned self-defense techniques and how to fight back against rapists.

But the paradox now to be grappled with is that upping women's awareness and anger about rape has also had the unintended—and probably not so beneficial—by-product effect of reinforcing conventional feminine fear and vulnerability, which also impedes women's lives, wending its way into every corner of female emotional existence, including the propensity for emotional injury by men. The question we're left to solve is how women are supposed to negotiate the psychical terrain of vulnerability in a social context where physical inviolability is hardly guaranteed, and when it's a bodily fact that sexual violation and sexual pleasure share the same . . . venue. Who wouldn't get confused, politically and otherwise? The pop-feminist solution, endlessly commemorating Strong Women while treating ordinary men as equivalent to rapists when they're merely being (for instance) romantically disappointing, or watching porn, or having midlife crises, or being needy, pants-dropping, self-destructive presidential clowns—well how is that really helpful to anyone?

The fact is that men are far more likely than women to be crime victims: as of 2004, the rate of violent crime against men was twenty-five per thousand, for women it was eighteen per thousand, according to the Department of Justice. Yet women are the ones who fear crime more. Even when women *know* their risk of crime is lower than a man's, women still experience higher degrees of fear, fear that starts coloring everything else in life, making even relatively innocuous situations like being asked for money on the street or minor annoyances like getting an obscene phone call far more fear inducing, according to research on victimization fear. On the whole, women prove to be 87 percent more afraid of crime than men are, according to one such study.

Behind this paradox—researchers have determined and can demonstrate by means of elaborate graphs with headings like "plotted equations from analysis of covariance"—is, not so surprisingly, women's fear of being raped. Rape casts its sinister shadow over how women think about all crime, and the higher an individual woman perceives her risk of rape to be, the more generally fearful of crime she'll be. In other words, fear of rape colors all female social experience, leading to what the researchers call a "differential sensitivity to risk" between men and women. But interestingly, perceived risk turns out to be an entirely different matter than objective risk. It turns out that fear of crime actually has *no* relation to any objective measurements of crime: women in the Northeast have a higher fear of rape than women in other regions, even though the Northeast has a lower number of rapes than any other part of the country. Before criminologists figured this out, the presumption was that reducing crime would reduce fear of crime; this turns out not to be the case.

The primary factor affecting fear of crime isn't the statistical likelihood of it occurring; it's your *perception* of how likely it is to happen. Then there's a second variable: how serious you perceive the particular crime to be. Among women of all ages, the perceived seriousness of rape is worse than the perceived seriousness of murder—largely, it turns out, because women also vastly overestimate the likelihood of being murdered while being raped. In a

1989 study, women believed that on the average, at least 25 percent of rape victims were killed during rapes. The study's authors estimated that the likelihood was closer to 3 percent at the time.

The picture of crime in the United States has actually changed rather dramatically since then: violent crime has dropped about 57 percent in the last decade and is now at the lowest level since 1974, when the government started collecting national crime data. Rape and attempted rape are down by 75 percent. How likely is it that a woman in the United States is going to be raped and murdered these days? According to the FBI's Uniform Crime Report—and this may come as a surprise—36 women in this country were both raped and murdered in 2004. With 94,635 reported rapes and attempted rapes, this means that fewer than 1 in 2,500 rape victims was murdered.* Compare this figure to the 97 murders—of both sexes—of those involved in romantic

---

*Or 36 out of 108,950 rapes and attempted rapes according to the National Crime Victimization Survey (NCVS), which includes unreported crimes as well as male victims. The NCVS, which surveys crime victims over the age of twelve in a selection of representative households, says that around 10 percent of sexual assault victims are male, whereas the FBI's Uniform Crime Report (UCR) doesn't include men, defining rape as "the carnal knowledge of a female forcibly and against her will." The two Justice Department surveys use different methodologies and measure somewhat different populations: the UCR includes victims under twelve and the NCVS includes unreported crimes. Of course, the issue of unreported rapes makes all this data very uncertain. The NCVS says that only 36 percent of the rapes and sexual assaults in its survey were reported, except that if this figure is right, it would seem to make the UCR figures (94,635 reported rapes and attempted rapes) too high. Attempting to compare the two surveys brings on a fast attack of math anxiety; queries to the Bureau of Justice Statistics about the discrepancies produce friendly but complicated answers about rolling averages and composite numbers. In short, regard all these numbers (other than murder figures) as rough estimates at best.

triangles: clearly an activity that should generate far more trepidation than it does. By the way, when it comes to murder, you're actually more than twice as likely to kill yourself as to be killed by someone else, giving new weight to the old truism that you're your own worst enemy. There doesn't yet appear to be research on whether plummeting crime rates have diminished women's fear of rape, but all previous indications are that subjective vulnerability doesn't correlate to either objective risk or variables in risk.

Needless to say, there's been a *lot* of bitter debate about rape statistics over the years: disbelief about the notorious "one in four women has been raped" claim on the one side, charges of underreporting and malicious indifference to the true prevalence of rape on the other. Then you have tough-strutting types like Camille Paglia accusing the Take Back the Night crowd of not understanding how sex really works, or "the joy of violation and destruction." It's like, you know, animal. *Take me you brute, do it to me hard.* In the midst of which, TV crime dramas continue to offer a weekly parade of mutilated rape-murder victims, sexually sadistic serial killers run rampant in the movies, the newsroom motto is "If it bleeds, it leads," and you don't hear much about the declining number of rapes in the media *or* from activists. On the contrary, you may get the sense the rape data are spun to pump up fear. The activist group RAINN (Rape, Abuse, and Incest National Network), which bills itself as "the nation's largest anti-sexual assault organization," reports that in 2004 there were 204,370 sexual-assault victims (arriving at this number by rolling together the NCVS figures for rape, attempted rape, and sexual assault), warning direly that there's one victim of sexual assault every two and a half minutes somewhere in America. "Sexual assault" means any kind of unwanted sexual contact, from being groped to being flashed at. Being flashed may be unpleasant (or it may be laughable, depending on your sense of humor), but the emotional seriousness is going to depend on how finely honed your sense of vulnerability is, and your finely honed sense of vulnerability, as the research demonstrates, derives from exacerbating the likelihood of rape—a perception you're likely to absorb by reading rape-activist literature. Elsewhere in the RAINN materials you'll find an amendment to the effect that there were only 65,510 completed rapes (a figure that also includes male rapes); thus there's an actual rape only every eight minutes rather than every two and a half minutes. But even this could be dialed down, since another way of putting it is that your chance of being raped is less than two-tenths of a percent, which might make a girl feel a little less like a moving target. After all, as sociologist Mark Warr puts it, "When it comes to rape . . . a little risk goes a long way in producing fear."

So does rape-activism literature unwittingly collaborate in reinforcing traditional feminine socialization? Fear of rape is a woman's constant companion in these accounts, her best buddy. No one wants to say that rape isn't a social problem, and it remains a social problem, but as we see, at least it's less of a social problem than it's been, which is good news, right? However, you won't see this good news reflected in the literature. For instance, Ann J. Cahill's 2001 book *Rethinking Rape* neglects to rethink rape sufficiently to mention that rape has declined every year since 1992. Instead Cahill portrays the situation like this: "In a society where women are constantly threatened with rape . . ." And: "rape and the fear of rape are a daily part of every woman's consciousness." Is there a certain . . . reluctance to yield the position of female vulnerability? Note that in such passages (and Cahill's are hardly the only examples), rape and fear of rape have become entirely interchangeable. And this is precisely the emotional reality for women, according to the social scientists studying victimization fear.

But rape does remain "a threat which is disproportionately leveled against women as a class," as Cahill puts it. Or does it? It may come as a surprise to hear that as many men as women are probably raped every year in the United States, and possibly more. Okay, most of these men are incarcerated at the time—but it's still *rape.* Obviously the circumstances make precise numbers impossible to pin down, though so are precise data on nonprison rape. The figures on male prison rape look something like this: the U.S. prison population now exceeds an astounding 2.2 million, of which roughly 93 percent are men. According to studies by Human Rights Watch, a *conservative* estimate is that 20 percent of all inmates are sexually assaulted or forced into unwanted sex, and at least 7 percent are raped. Prison advocacy groups put the rape rate closer to 10 percent. A cautious estimate, conclude legal scholars Robert Weisberg and

David Mills, is that nearly 200,000 inmates have been raped. Meanwhile, in the (ever-shrinking) noncustodial population, rape and sexual assault are at all-time lows.

It's impossible to put nonincarcerated and incarcerated rates of rape side by side, since we have annual figures in one case and experiences that are often repeated or ongoing in the other, but the picture of who's most susceptible to rape in the United States is clearly shifting, and clearly male rape is an entrenched feature of the American social fabric. Given the staggering size of the U.S. prison population (including local jails and juvenile facilities), the number of men who are targeted is huge. It begins to look as though the most sexually vulnerable population in America at this point in history is not women, it's the incarcerated—well over half of whom are nonviolent offenders, by the way, thanks to mandatory drug sentencing. Of course, women inmates are also particularly vulnerable— overrepresented as sex-abuse victims, though making up only 7 percent of the inmate population. Rape statistics on incarcerated women are even more impossible to pin down, since the abusers are frequently prison staff, both male and female.

The general view of male prison rape seems to be that it isn't comparable to what women experience, or at least it doesn't matter in the same way, because . . . it happened in prison. In fact, it's often the subject of nervous hilarity on late-night talk shows and in stand-up comedy of the male-sexual-anxiety genre: get stopped for running a red light and next thing you know, you've made a new best friend. Just don't bend over in the shower, dude! Maybe prison rape is a more jocular subject than nonprison rape because those affected are mostly criminals and thus deserve it—criminals who also tend to be minorities (60 percent) and members of the underclass, possibly tacitly adding to the indifference, or the potential for humor. Nonincarcerated women who are raped are tragic victims; those raped in prison— well, "If you can't do the time . . ."

Even if only right-wing radio hosts say this kind of thing out loud, a certain callousness prevails, and even feminists writing about rape are a bit indifferent. Susan Brownmiller is an exception, though she doesn't let the fact of male rape affect her overall analysis; instead she gets tied up in contradictions trying to decide whether prison rape is homosexual or not. Most discussions of male prison rape conclude with convoluted explanations to the effect that prison rapists don't actually want to rape men; they'd *prefer* to be raping women. In other words, the pervasiveness of male prison rape somehow ends up underlining the fact that females are the "normal" victims of rape, and thus remain the designated sexually vulnerable population. The Justice Department collaborates by not including prison rape in its annual crime surveys, eliminating it as a social issue by statistical fiat.

Then came the 2003 Prison Rape Elimination Act—signed by President George W. Bush (flanked by two male former inmates who'd been raped in prison) and enacted by Congress—which provided $60 million for a two-year survey to be conducted by the Bureau of Justice Statistics. Which is to say that the Prison

Rape Elimination Act proposed to *measure* prison rape, not eliminate it. As critics like Weisberg and Mills point out, this is both quixotic and redundant, given that Human Rights Watch had already compiled as much data as anyone was going to under the circumstances. The first BJS report, issued in 2005, is an elaborate joke. After surveying 1.7 million inmates, or 79 percent of adults and juveniles in custody, the report cites 8,210 allegations of sexual violence, and a full 2,090 of these were found to be "substantiated."

Given the vast number of male prison rapes and the declining number of female nonprison rapes, it seems as though the larger social story about sexual vulnerability is due to be altered. It is, after all, a story upon which a good chunk of contemporary gender identity hinges, including a large part of what it *feels* like to be a woman: endangered. It's been argued by feminists that patriarchy requires the female body to be vulnerable—that is, by definition, penetrable—in part so as to leave men under the illusion that they're not (at least for those who eschew this kind of thing). Which may be one reason male prison rape is tacitly permitted: everyone knows it happens, but there are a lot of reasons to disavow that it means anything. Even feminists writing on the subject have some conceptual difficulty here. Ann Cahill, in *Rethinking Rape,* is aware of the prevalence of prison rape but still manages to write, "Relatively few men face rape." She can only mean relatively few middle-class white men, since some 30 percent of black men these days are going to spend time in jail. (The United States imprisons black men at a rate approximately four times the imprisonment rate of black men in South Africa under apartheid, a rate that will soon produce a prison population that equals the number of black men enslaved at the height of American slavery.)

If there's been an unjust distribution of fear and insecurity between the sexes historically, at least there's increasing evidence that a more equitable distribution of sexual vulnerability now pertains. Unfortunately, it doesn't yet extend to the non-incarcerated male population. Also unfortunately, there's no perfect eye-for-an-eye system of justice in which men who rape outside prison will get raped once inside. But if you don't have to be biologically female to become a rape victim and if being biologically male really isn't a guarantee of inviolability against unwanted penetration, would this new math, if it filtered into general social consciousness, go some way toward reconstituting the gendered psyche? If rape were finally construed as an equal-opportunity form of victimization, would the social script about what women *are* and *feel* be instantly transformed, along with all the impeding and contagious varieties of female vulnerability, given that rape is the paradigmatic vulnerability fear?

The question remains whether rape is a symptom of phallic masculinity, as feminists have charged, or if this blows everything out of proportion, and men really aren't so bad, as anti-feminists like Christina Hoff Sommers *(Who Stole Feminism?*

How Women Have Betrayed Women) argue. Poor guys—they're just misunderstood by hairy-legged man-hating types. Sommers thinks that rape actually has nothing to do with gender at all: women aren't raped because they're women, they're raped because there are bad people out there. "Rape is perpetrated by criminals . . . people who are wont to gratify themselves in criminal ways." Ironically, Sommers is so busy scratching and kicking at those she calls "gender feminists" that she ends up sketching quite a radical gender position herself without quite noticing, since in this rather visionary account of a world where gender doesn't exist and misogyny is a feminist invention, what prevents marauding gangs of criminally minded women from finding smallish men, holding them down, and penetrating them digitally or with other implements? (Not all male rapists rely on their own appendages either.) It's an interesting prospect to consider. Besides which, female violence *is* on the rise nationwide, and feminists have frequently argued that rape isn't about sex, it's about violence. In fact, according to the 2005 BJS prison abuse report, 67 percent of perpetrators of *substantiated* prison staff sexual misconduct were female, as were 14 of the instances involving nonconsensual sexual acts with prisoners. (No further elaboration on the specifics unfortunately, about which one would definitely like to know more.) Way to go on the gender equality, ladies, since there's nothing more fanciful than the idea that women, once in positions of power, would act more humanely or more virtuously than men. If in doubt, recall the photos of female soldiers at Abu Ghraib. The sentimental premise that something in female nature is inherently gentle is a social fiction comparable to the one about only women being vulnerable to rape. But are women themselves actually willing to give up on either?

The evidence so far is mixed. Interestingly, as the number of female rapes have declined, new forms of sexual vulnerability have ascended to social prominence. Take professor-student relationships, that burning academic question of the day. Where once the issue was coercion or quid pro quo sex *("Let's talk about how you can improve your grade, Ms. Jones. Come to my office at six.")*, with the popularity of the sex-as-injury script, now it's any whiff of eros across the generations. The premise that such situations are invariably exploitative has become the new propriety, with colleges around the country devising complex regulatory codes often banning relationships between *any* professor and *any* student, not only those the professor grades. Note that this requires a large dose of amnesia about all the professors still on the faculty married to former students, a few even happily. But since such encounters can't be *guaranteed* to turn out well—as if the majority of romantic encounters do—new regulations are needed to protect students from possible romantic adversity or getting treated badly in predictable ways. To further protect students, these new campus harassment codes also routinely warn professors against creating any kind of "offensive environment,"

particularly situations that might cause a student to "experience his or her vulnerability," in or out of the classroom. (Isn't experiencing your vulnerability pretty much the definition of sentience?) Prepare for a shock: the vulnerability of students has hardly decreased under the new paradigm; it's increasing by the second; since as the definition of injury keeps expanding, so do opportunities to *feel* injured. Students are now encouraged to regard themselves as such exquisitely sensitive creatures that an errant classroom remark impedes their education, such hothouse flowers that an unfunny joke creates a lasting trauma, and will land the unfunny prof in the dean's office or, occasionally, on the national news.

No doubt we'd all benefit from more self-knowledge about sex, and someday soon the miracle drug will be invented that cures the abyss between desire and intelligence. Well, let's hope. In the meantime, the hot new category of offense sweeping campuses and workplaces is the "unwanted sexual advance." Goodness, what tangled tales of backfired desires, bristling umbrage, and mutual misunderstanding lurk behind this sterile little phrase! In the right hands, such narratives would no doubt provide great raw material for satire: look how obtuse humans can be when in the throes of desire; what eternal optimists about our charms and physical allures! Unfortunately, those deploying this unwieldy coinage find nothing remotely funny in such situations. Forget bumbling pathos or social ineptitude—in these accounts, the protagonists are traumatized, the antagonists small-time sex criminals. But wait, how are you supposed to know your advance is unwanted until you try—do we all wear our desires written in neon letters on our foreheads? Besides which, desire is hardly such a stable condition to begin with—surely one is occasionally caught by surprise, unexpectedly propelled from nondesire into raging lust by something in the moment, or the air, or the wine?

Recent literary treatments of the student-professor theme are far less optimistic about the possibilities for sexual reform than the crowd behind the new regulations. In J. M. Coetzee's *Disgrace*, Francine Prose's *Blue Angel*, David Mamet's *Oleanna*, to name just a few, if one thing is clear it's that learning has an inverse relationship to self-knowledge and that professors are invariably emblems of sexual stupidity. Frankly, it's hard to have much conviction about rectifying the condition. If colleges really wanted to enlighten students, the students are the ones who should get the mandatory sex-harassment workshops, not their teachers. For instance: "Ten Signs That Your Professor Is Sleeping with You to Assuage Midlife Depression and Will Dump You Shortly Afterward" or "Will Hooking Up With a Prof Really Make You Feel Smarter: Pros and Cons."*

If anything has made recent feminism irrelevant and ridiculous, it's this reductiveness about desire and the embrace of victimology, a tendency which reached its apex in a 2004 *New York*

---

*Just to be clear, *ongoing* unwanted sexual advances—or threats or quid pro quo demands—otherwise known as "sexual harassment," should be subject to the most severe punishment, including loss of livelihood, property seizure, and potential incarceration.

magazine cover story by Naomi Wolf, who created an international media stir by recounting a long-ago unwanted sexual advance. The stir was because the advancer happened to be literary lion Harold Bloom—a man of rather advanced years by the time of Wolf's accusations—who had "sexually encroached" on her, she charged, some twenty years before, when she was a student.

The story, worth some attention given its emblematic qualities, went like this: In 1983, Wolf was in her senior year at Yale and Bloom was one of its celebrity professors, "a vortex of power and intellectual charisma." He had an aura that was compelling and intimidating, he attracted brilliant acolytes, and Wolf wanted to be one of them, drawn to him intellectually but also terrifically scared of him: when he invited her to come chat with him after she'd audited one of his famous courses, she was "sick with excitement" at the prospect. Boy, you sense the trouble brewing already—it's like an Ivy League version of a bodice ripper, the only missing element is the somewhat rotund Bloom galloping across campus astride a white steed. Overcoming her tremors, Wolf asks Bloom if she can do an independent study devoted to critiquing her poetry; the great man agrees to meet with the fledgling poet weekly. Unfortunately, these sessions fail to come off. Bloom, known for hanging out with his student coterie at a local pub, suggests getting together over a glass of amontillado to discuss the poems; this never happens either. Eventually he invites himself over to dinner one night with Wolf and her two roommates—one of the roommates happened to be

Bloom's editorial assistant. After dinner—during which everyone drinks a lot of Bloom's amontillado—the roommates go off
somewhere, Bloom and Wolf are sitting on the couch. Bloom
clutches the manuscript close. Wolf thinks she's finally going to
receive a few pearls of insight from the illustrious scholar. Instead he leans over, breathing, "You have the aura of election
upon you." Then he *puts his hand on her thigh*—a "heavy, bone-
less hand," as Wolf describes it, in a bit of literary-anatomical
flourish that brings other appendages to mind. Wolf leaps up
and vomits into the kitchen sink. Bloom leaps up and gets his
coat, corks up the rest of his fancy sherry, and leaves, telling her,
"You are a deeply troubled girl." They never meet again; Bloom
gives her a B for the independent study.

   "Once you have been sexually encroached upon by a professor, your faith in your work corrodes," writes Wolf. The hand-
on-knee incident provoked a "moral crisis": Wolf lost faith in
Yale as an institution because it tacitly *sanctioned* this kind of behavior, she believed, and she never wrote any more poetry. Even
so, Bloom is not really a "bad man"; actually, he's a complex and
brilliant man, and no more demonic than any other complex
human being, but this doesn't *excuse* him. It doesn't let Yale off
the hook either, and Wolf says she's coming forward at this
late date only because Yale officials wouldn't return her phone
calls about the matter for months on end, then she got a big
runaround, and when an administration higher-up finally did
get on the phone, he refused to act on a twenty-year-old charge.
It's not actually clear that Bloom's groping violated university

policy at the time: in 1983 the terminology of the unwanted sexual advance had yet to be invented, though under Yale's current harassment codes, would-be Blooms will find themselves in hot water. Despite these now-well-publicized strictures and prohibitions, Wolf maintains that Yale and similar academic institutions still tacitly sanction harassment; thus she's compelled to expose the situation—and the reprobate Bloom—in the national media, so that students today won't have to go through what she went through. Also because of her *shame* over her own cowardice: given her failure to tell the truth about what really goes on at Yale up until now, Wolf detects in herself "that soft spot of complicity," and she's not at peace in her mind when the sun sets on the Jewish day of atonement. It's on her shoulders.

Now, all this is a shade self-dramatizing, but can we say that it's self-dramatizing in a particularly *feminine* way? The idioms employed have that feminist ring, but it's a genre of feminism dedicated to revivifying an utterly traditional femininity: woundedbird femininity, to borrow Joan Didion's useful formulation. It's not just that in the midst of the many protests about how awful it all was, eroticism perfumes the air; it's also that this massive overinvestment in paternal figures and institutions has such a distinctly Oedipal flavor. The contradiction of Wolf-style devoted-daughter feminism is its thralldom to the phallic mythos it's also so deeply offended by. *Why* was Wolf "sick with excitement" when Bloom summoned her for a chat? Precisely because he was a charismatic and famous guy, because she desired his approval and wanted him to find her attractive, as she di-

147

vulges in her 1997 memoir, *Promiscuities*—in other words, she desired something from him in some impossibly conflicted way, that may not have been precisely the way he desired her. And let's face it: the sexual privilege that accrues to Important Men like Bloom accrues for exactly this sort of reason. But ascribing these kinds of scenes to male sexual rapaciousness alone doesn't really tell the whole story. Or the truth. For one thing, it conveniently leaves female desire out of the story. Paradoxically, the trouble really starts when the idealized masculine icon fails to be phallic *enough,* as invariably happens—after all, the phallus *is* only a myth.* The problem is when the icons turn out to be flawed and insecure themselves, when it turns out that Big Men also want validation from those they're supposed to validate. And with so much father worship driving the story, how could the fathers involved not fail and disappoint, most likely in some way having to do with sex? The real question about the phallus these days is whether it's something men try to put over on women or whether women endow men with phallic prowess in order to keep desiring—and disdaining—them.

On which point—the point being repetition scenarios—why is it that Wolf is so compelled to keep publicly returning to this encroachment scene? She'd previously fictionalized the same

---

*An old Freud joke:

FREUD: Anna, although I am your father, as part of your education I must show you my penis so you understand certain fundamental concepts. Now, do you see the difference between the penis and the phallus?

ANNA: Yes, Father. The penis is like the phallus, only much smaller.

episode in *Promiscuities*, where Bloom appears as "Dr. Johnson." What's next, the Broadway musical? Absent from either account is any shred of recognition that the recipients of such advances, gross and unpleasant as they may be, wield just a tiny bit of power too—the power to reject and humiliate the advancer, at the very least. Wolf may begrudge Bloom's attempts to employ her for grubby purposes of masculine validation, but then what she's resenting, ironically, *is* the fact that she has power over him too. Yes, for her good looks and youth, but they're hardly worthless currency in our culture, no doubt especially so for those whom nature has chosen to deprive in this regard. And, sure, Bloom has power over her because of his fame and literary prowess, not his movie-star visage or buff physique—and not just because he was collecting a paycheck from Yale. The levels of mutual misrecognition here approach the level of farce—it was probably fortunate those student poems of Wolf's went unread, since it's also hard to imagine two more alien sensibilities. What isn't clear is that either one's fantasy was any more objectifying than the other.

A friendly hint to future unwanted-advance recipients: power does come in more than one guise. There's the power of public shame, for instance, and the power of underlings to humiliate and humble their superiors, and even if this is the subtext of Wolf's late-in-the-day reprisal, and though women humiliating men is a theme that propels some of the great books and movies of our time (and perhaps the occasional *New York* magazine piece), somehow Wolf manages to be quite insensible on the subject of her own power, or her own capacity for aggression. Instead we get all this injured nobility and sisterhood.

Another latent cultural script animates this story, of course: note the metaphors of downfall that pervade it, as if being advanced on sexually were somehow socially lowering. Wolf said that the one-time advance by Bloom caused her grades to drop, caused her faith in herself and her work to plummet, devastated her sense of being valuable to Yale as anything but a pawn of powerful men, and "corrupted" her entire educational experience. When Paula Jones brought suit against former president Bill Clinton for the one-time unwanted sexual advance she said he made while governor of Arkansas, she used the same language: she claimed she'd suffered a potential "loss of reputation." *Down, down, down.*

Obviously sex has a thorny relation to questions of social hierarchy in our culture: traditionally coded as socially "low," and located in the lower body rather than the more elevated regions like the brain, it's symbolically assigned to the lower rungs of the social-class stepladder. The same goes for pornography, the lowest form of "low culture," and displays of sexuality in public, often considered "low-class." Being caught in improper sexual situations is likewise socially demoting. In contrast, what's associated with the upper body is coded as socially elevated: cognition, rationality, the soul. It's all deeply familiar, and you really hate seeing feminists (even opportunity feminists à la Paula Jones) recycling such hoary stuff, not only because of all the assumptions about class it smuggles into the social conversation, but also because it's the same symbolic logic that once operated against rape victims (and still does in some cultures), in which a sexual transgression socially demotes the victim. In traditional cultures, women who are raped are still sometimes killed to protect family honor.

As we see, underneath public testimonies about sexual encroachment can lurk some tangled agendas. And here's another utterly tangled example to contemplate. A few years before Wolf's story appeared, another prominent feminist, Andrea Dworkin, published her own rather problematical sexual-violation story, which appeared simultaneously in the *Guardian*, a British paper, and the *New Statesman*, a magazine. It too created an international stir. As with Wolf's, it was a retrospective account: a harrowing story about what had happened, Dworkin said, in a Paris hotel the previous year.

Dworkin, fifty-two at the time, was on her second Kir Royale in the hotel garden, reading a book, when she suddenly felt sick and weak. The second drink hadn't tasted right. She staggered up to her room and collapsed on the bed. The bartender's assistant—the one who'd served her the drink—brought up the dinner she'd ordered earlier from room service; then she passed out. When she awoke, four or five hours later, it was night, and she was in pain. "I hurt deep inside my vagina. . . . I went to the toilet and found blood on my right hand, fresh, bright red, not menstrual blood, not clotted blood. I'm past bleeding. I tried to find the source of the blood. My hand got covered in it again." She also found deep, bleeding gashes on her leg, and a strange bruise on her left breast that looked like a bite mark. She began to think that she'd been drugged and raped, and she thought the bartender had probably done it—alerted that she'd passed out by the assistant—because the bartender had made the drinks and had "flirted grandly with me, though I had not reciprocated." She didn't know if the assistant had been there for the rape also, but thought probably yes. More speculations follow: maybe the two had pulled her down toward the bottom of the bed so that her vagina would be near the bed's edge and her legs more easy to manipulate—but how had the assistant gotten into her room in the first place, since the door had been dead-bolted and he'd appeared suddenly, already inside? Since she couldn't stand the thought of making a wrong allegation, she didn't seek medical help, or go to the police, or even call hotel security.

To say that the account had a rather hallucinatory quality doesn't quite capture the flavor.

Dworkin, who died in 2005 at age fifty-eight, was a writer who'd always used autobiography as her moral touchstone, in books like *Intercourse,* which argued in wonderfully inflamed prose, that sexual penetration is a paradigm of oppression even when consensual. "Intercourse remains a means, or the means, of physiologically making a woman inferior: communicating to her, cell by cell, her own inferior status . . . pushing and thrusting until she gives in." All her books make pretty much this argument, it must be said—the sexual disgust they convey is really quite powerful. The disgust is all displaced onto men, however: men are disgusted by women and fuck them because they hate them. Semen also has contaminating qualities, and Dworkin believed men use semen to make women dirty: "In literary pornography, to ejaculate is to *pollute* the woman." Semen is "driven into [the woman] to dirty her or make her more dirty or make her dirty by him." The hatred seems pretty mutual actually, though Dworkin could also be kind of funny about it: "In seduction, the rapist often bothers to buy a bottle of wine."

In *Scapegoat: The Jews, Israel, and Women's Liberation*—published in the United Kingdom a week after the rape account appeared—we read in the book's opening paragraphs about beatings and torture Dworkin suffered in her marriage thirty years before. Dworkin's was a biography that included the full menu of sexual victimization, beginning with a sexual molestation at age nine in a movie theater—though she wasn't legally raped, as she clarified in one essay, "since fingers and a hand were used for penetration, not the officially requisite penis." She married a Dutch anarchist, an "assassin," who battered her for five years, beating her with planks and burning her breasts with cigarettes, until she finally escaped, aided by a feminist friend, and went into hiding: still, "every trip outside might mean death if he found me." She'd worked as a prostitute, trading sex for shelter and food: more abuse and violence. In 1965 she was arrested at an antiwar demonstration, then assaulted by the two male prison doctors during a brutal internal examination. "They pretty much tore me up inside with a steel speculum and had themselves a fine old time verbally tormenting me as well."

Her experiences at the hands of men have been beyond horrible, and Dworkin always presented her own life as paradigmatic of the female condition. Which is to say that if you believe the biography, you have to believe that men are a demonic race whose main purpose is to victimize and exploit women's vulnerability by means of sex.

What made the latest rape all the more horrific was being knocked out with drugs first: "This rape was necrophiliac: they wanted to fuck a dead woman." The drugs stole her memory of the event. "It was horrible not knowing. I had literally no memory of what the man and the boy had done. It's like being operated on. You don't feel anything until you feel the pain that comes with a return to consciousness. I speculated that my body must have been relaxed, no muscles straining, no physical resistance or even tension. This repelled me." Reflecting on the sheer ease of sexual assault aided by so-called date-rape drugs, Dworkin writes, "You can do this hundreds of times with virtually no chance of getting caught, let alone having anyone be able to make a legal case in any court of law." Studies on rape and pornography quote 30 percent of men as saying they'd rape if they could get away with it; citing this, Dworkin concludes that with amnesiac drugs like these, now they can: it's foolproof rape. In other words, rape is now just about entirely inescapable.

Reactions to Dworkin's story ranged from horror and sympathy to pity and disbelief. Articles soon appeared gingerly raising doubts about the veracity and the details. No one wanted to be in the position of doubting a rape victim's story, but how could both the bartender and his assistant be absent from their duties in the hotel without incurring questions? How did the assistant get into the room if the door was dead-bolted? And how could a longtime antirape activist not inform the police or hotel security when she realized what had happened to her—were the bartender and his accomplice to be allowed to continue drugging and raping female guests, if indeed they had? There was also the ineluctable . . . *strangeness* of the telling, including Dworkin's self-flagellating questions about why the rapists had selected her in the first place. "I go down the checklist," Dworkin writes. "No short skirt; it was daylight; I didn't drink a lot even though it was alcohol and I rarely drink, but so what? It could have been Wild Turkey or coffee. I didn't drink with a man, I sat alone and read a book, I didn't go somewhere I shouldn't have been, wherever that might be when you are 52, I didn't flirt, I didn't want it to happen. I wasn't hungry for a good, hard fuck that would leave me pummeled with pain inside." Aren't these just the sort of questions that feminist activists have spent decades contesting—along with the premise that women who get raped did something to deserve it?

Then there were accusations that given the timing of the article, the whole thing was a publicity stunt to get attention for the new book. Was Dworkin deliberately telling a questionable story, playing the feminist martyr whose agonized cries are never believed? "It reads almost as if Dworkin wants to be doubted," wrote one skeptic nervously. But even Dworkin's longtime critics thought the idea of a rape-charge publicity stunt was too cynical. "I could easily believe she had a black-out, and nasty injuries, from an unexpected dose of alcohol and sunburn," wrote Susie Bright, a frequent antagonist. But Bright also concluded that Dworkin had just lost her mind. "As I read Andrea's confession, tears came to my eyes. . . . Let's put the rape story aside—I don't have to ascertain whether Dworkin has been assaulted on this occasion or not. She is hurting, and something is wrong." The skeptics included Dworkin's partner of thirty years, gay feminist John Stoltenberg (they were a platonic couple, though they eventually married; Dworkin described him as a "non-genital man"). For reasons of her own, Dworkin decided to announce her partner's doubts to the world: "John looked for any other explanation than rape. He abandoned me emotionally. Now a year has passed and sometimes he's with me in his heart and sometimes not."

After Dworkin returned to New York following the Europe trip, she fell seriously ill—at one point she was found wandering the streets of New York, delirious with a fever, and was hospitalized. This led to speculation that Dworkin, dangerously overweight and unwieldy, might have had a similar episode in the Paris hotel—might have fallen and maybe cut and bruised herself. Of course, Dworkin's own work predicted such questions. Elsewhere she'd written about rape victims, "There is always a problem for a woman: being believed." If Dworkin's work turned out to be the classic self-fulfilling prophesy, she did always proffer her own life as exemplary of the female situation. Which makes this whole painful story one that can't fail to raise certain thorny questions about the contours of female emotional life, and makes Dworkin still such a gripping—and symptomatic—figure. (Well, gripping in the sense that she makes you want to look away.)

Dworkin was quite fascinated by rape, and somehow what she most feared . . . kept happening. As she wrote following the latest rape: "I study it. I read about it. I think about it . . . I was raped before this. I remember being raped . . . I know hundreds if not thousands of raped women." There's no doubt that Dworkin's was a life of pain; it's what fueled her driven, often compelling loopiness. She suffered along with all the ravaged, bruised, mutilated women who people her books, also demanding to be accepted as representative females. Dworkin tells their stories with a rather unseemly relish: she really loved writing about abjection. And seemed to get a certain pleasure from it—almost as much pleasure as she thought men took in causing it. Still, you have to admire the contrarian nerve of a woman who takes on the whole institution of sexual intercourse. As Susie Bright (no sexual shrinking violet) put it in her blog, eulogizing Dworkin, "There is something about literally being fucked that colors your world, pretty or ugly, and it was about time someone said so." The problem is that it's never entirely clear when reading Dworkin whether intercourse sexually subordinates women in the context of a sexist society, or whether it always will. Is she making a political argument, or describing the eternal feminine condition? The aversion to penetration runs so deep and the idea of pleasure is so absent, it's hard to say.

What's peculiarly striking in Dworkin's account of female experience is how close it comes to the most orthodox Freudian conceptions of femininity, which also align the feminine with passivity. As with her pal MacKinnon, it's really a little confounding to find, smack at the epicenter of American radical feminism, all the most repudiated concepts emerging in the subtext of the story. What seems to keep popping up is the affinity of femininity and masochism; the element of satisfaction in suffering and humiliation. It's the old Freudian narrative, this time around relocated from inner life to social life and projected outward.*

Dworkin's central idea that sexual subordination is enforced by sexual intercourse is also awfully reminiscent of one of Freud's most devoted female adherents, Helene Deutsch, who was roundly trashed by subsequent female psychoanalysts and feminists for her biologism—the usual criticism is that she overemphasized the physical basis of the female experience. (Juliet Mitchell's 1974 *Psychoanalysis and Feminism,* which re-

---

*Though Freud, who also believed in an inherent bisexuality, doesn't get enough credit for the idea that all humans vacillate between masculine and feminine positions, between activity and passivity. It never increased his popularity with feminist critics at least, who just dislike what gets assigned to the feminine side of the equation. Freud's argument was that he didn't do the assigning; culture did.

introduced Freud to feminists, is especially tough on Deutsch.) Deutsch's crime was to point out that the female experience of sexuality *is* often painful: menstruation and childbirth involve pain; turning toward men for sexual gratification is, in the first instance, painful. "Defloration"—what a way to be ushered into the joys of womanhood! How could there not be consequences to the female psyche from such bodily experiences, Deutsch asked? (Like Freud, Deutsch too had a tragic sense of the human; she wasn't looking only for cheery news.) Deutsch further speculated, based on her clinical experience with female patients, that women protect themselves from the dangers of this unconscious masochism through narcissism. This may sound a little unflattering—though it's also a point you're likely to arrive at yourself after reading the violation testimonies of Wolf and Dworkin, which shuttle so flamboyantly between the two modes. And what would Deutsch make of the recent crop of self-dramatizing literary sexual confessionals, you wonder— *The Sexual Life of Catherine M* or Toni Bentley's *The Surrender: An Erotic Memoir,* and the slew of less well-done examples— obsessive feminine masochism infused with the ecstasy of public self-exposure: a perfect storm of high-profile narcissism, wrapped in an invitation for social rebuke. (Note that in the variation known as "social masochism," society itself is solicited to mete out the desired punishment, in lieu of the usual sadist. Or perhaps in this case, book critics.) Sounding much like Deutsch herself, Toni Bentley poses this question about her sexual adventures: "Why was the pain so very interesting? It felt as though the key to my soul was buried inside it." It's the question Dworkin never managed to ask.

The premise that masochism is either an inevitable part of female sexuality or somehow inherently "feminine"—even when experienced by men (as it often is)—was always one of the big feminist bugaboos about the Freudian conception of female development. Which makes it really so curious to find contemporary victim narratives like Wolf's and Dworkin's reconfiguring feminist testimony into flashy public displays that so insistently smuggle in these old repudiated concepts, like devoted public dieters with a secret cache of candy in the desk drawer, sneaking bites of the forbidden substance. If somehow *even feminism itself*—the rescue program! the cure!—gets enlisted at the level of the female psyche to prop up the traditional femininity, to provide the cover story for an erotic identification with violation, well, this really *is* quite a female predicament.

That rape is both true and a fantasy definitely complicates things. What an outcry there was when Nancy Friday cataloged women's rape fantasies in her 1973 book *My Secret Garden*. "Rape does for a woman's sexual fantasy what the first martini does for her in reality: Both relieve her of responsibility and guilt. . . . She gets him to do what she wants him to do, while seeming to be forced," Friday writes. Which isn't so far from Dworkin's descriptions of being drugged and raped: rape is so *easy* for men now, and there's *nothing* you can do to avoid it. The position that unfurls in Dworkin's work and psyche (on parade enough of the time to allow the assessment) is that not being victimized somehow ceases to be possible. Note the slippage from the premise that some women get raped and that's a terrible thing to the premise that rape is inevitable. Note the slippage, in other words, from activism into fantasy.

Sure there can be pleasure in writing and thinking about being raped, or taken by force, or violated, or "encroached on." And if encroachment testimonies by leading feminists barrel into the media tinged with a certain amount of subterfuge and literary embellishment, even as the testifier claims to be speaking "the real," well, who really knows her own motives and desires so thoroughly when it comes to fantasy? Self-knowledge can be in short supply—not that it's so overwhelmingly present elsewhere, needless to say. But more to the point, there's a political question that seems to get lost in all the confusion: Alongside the dedication to fighting violation, isn't what gets lost some notion of emancipation? Somehow the story always returns to subjugation instead. (Though if subjugation can have an erotic element, would this be where things get bottlenecked?)

To say that Dworkin got a bit unhinged about the whole penetration thing isn't to deny that violent things happen to women. Let's not forget that violent things happen to men too: they're maimed or die in pointless wars, for instance. Of course, then they become "casualties" or heroes rather than victims—the cultural script is entirely different. Dworkin didn't read the culture wrong: it's entirely true that all our idioms for penetration—"getting fucked," "screwed over"—are about humiliation and exploitation. Which does make it hard to see how anyone really *can* avoid a certain duality about the experience, even when it's pleasurable (as it often is!). Dworkin is the great case study in the ambivalence of femininity: after all, she's hardly *indifferent* about penetration. She may not have engaged in it voluntarily (she's on record as an abstainer), but can there be this much aversion without some corner of desire? The opposite of desire isn't aversion, it's indifference; it's the ability to not pay attention. There's no inattention here.

Reading Wolf and Dworkin side by side prompts certain not-so-acceptable speculations, particularly if you read them as exemplary narratives. If there's something in the female psyche—as currently constituted—that finds an element of gratification in the fantasy of "encroachment," that gravitates toward such mental scenarios, to what degree has this also underwritten the political calculations of contemporary feminism?

The premise that subordination has been imposed on women obviously isn't wrong, but it's only a partial explanation. The more contentious part of the story is the extent to which both femininity and feminism end up entangled in the same scenarios and repetitions. Or as Sylvia Plath put it a little pointedly in "Daddy":

> Every woman adores a Fascist.
> The boot in the face, the brute
> Brute heart of a brute like you.

In other words, when it comes to what men have and what women want from them—in public, in private—a detour through the subterranean, not-always-progressive recesses of the symbolic imagination has already happened, long before the public demands and position statements. Traces of the journey linger, nowhere more than in the myriad impasses of the female condition.

A full accounting of the female situation at the moment would need to start roughly here.

ACKNOWLEDGMENTS

Thank you to Yaddo, and to Northwestern University's School of Communication for a one-year Van Zelst Research Chair, during which I researched this book, and for an additional year of leave to write it—my gratitude to Dean Barbara O'Keefe. Thanks to Rebecca Mead and George Prochnik for inspiring discussions of Dirt and Sex, Meghan O'Rourke at *Slate*, where some early bits of this appeared, and to Lawrence Weschler. Many thanks to Beth Vesel, and Erroll McDonald, again. And to T. Spencer.

BIBLIOGRAPHY

Sources are listed in the chapter in which they first appear.

ENVY

Blyth, Myrna. *Spin Sisters: How the Women of the Media Sell Unhappiness—and Liberalism—to the Women of America*. New York: St. Martin's-Griffin, 2004.

Deutsch, Claudia H. "Behind the Exodus of Executive Women: Boredom." *New York Times,* May 1, 2005.

Dowd, Maureen. *Are Men Necessary? When Sexes Collide*. New York: Putnam, 2005.

Echols, Alice. *Daring to Be Bad: Radical Feminism in America, 1967–75*. Minneapolis: University of Minnesota Press, 1989.

Ehrenreich, Barbara, and Dierdre English. *For Her Own Good: 150 Years of the Experts' Advice to Women*. Garden City, N.Y.: Anchor Books, 1979.

Ensler, Eve. *The Good Body*. New York: Villard, 2004.

Friedan, Betty. *The Feminine Mystique*. New York: Dell, 1963.

Freud, Sigmund. "Female Sexuality." 1931. Translated and reprinted in *Standard Edition,* vol. 21, pp. 223–43. London: Hogarth Press, 1961.

———. "Femininity." 1933. Translated and reprinted in *Standard Edition,* vol. 22, pp. 112–35. London: Hogarth Press, 1964.

———. *Three Essays on the Theory of Sexuality*. 1905. Translated and reprinted in *Standard Edition,* vol. 7, pp. 125–245. London: Hogarth Press, 1905.

Fukuyama, Francis. *The Great Disruption: Human Nature and the Reconstitution of Social Order*. New York: Free Press, 2000.

Gallup Organization. *Gender and Society: Status and Stereotypes*. Princeton, N.J., 1996.

Gilbert, Neil. "Family Life: Sold on Work." *Society,* March–April 2005, 12–17.

Holland, Joshua. "Womenomics 101." *AlterNet,* March 16, 2006.

Johnston, David Kay. "Corporate Wealth Share Rises for Top-Income Americans." *New York Times,* January 29, 2006.

Leonhardt, David. "Poverty in U.S. Grew in 2004, While Income Failed to Rise for 5th Straight Year." *New York Times,* August 31, 2005.

Mayer, Elizabeth Lloyd. " 'Everybody Must Be Just Like Me': Observations on Female Castration Anxiety." *International Journal of Psycho-Analysis* 66 (1985): 331–37.

Newman, Judith. "The Devil and Miss Regan." *Vanity Fair,* January 2005.

Nietzsche, Friedrich. *On the Genealogy of Morals.* Translated by Walter Kaufmann. New York: Vintage, 1969.

Rhoads, Steven E. *Taking Sex Differences Seriously.* New York: Encounter Books, 2005.

Scott, Joan W. "Universalism and the History of Feminism." *Differences* 7, no. 1 (1995): 1–15.

Uchitelle, Louis. "Gaining Ground on the Wage Front." *New York Times,* December 31, 2004.

Wollstonecraft, Mary. *Vindication of the Rights of Woman.* 1792. Reprint, New York: Penguin, 1975.

SEX

Bair, Dierdre. *Simone de Beauvoir: A Biography.* New York: Touchstone, 1991.

Beauvoir, Simone de. *The Second Sex.* 1952. Reprint, New York: Vintage, 1989.

Dinnerstein, Dorothy. *The Mermaid and the Minotaur: Sexual Arrangements and Human Malaise.* New York: Harper & Row, 1976.

Douglass, Marcia, and Lisa Douglass. *The Sex You Want: A Lovers' Guide to Women's Sexual Pleasure.* New York: Marlowe & Company, 1997.

Eyer, Diane E. *Mother-Infant Bonding: A Scientific Fiction.* New Haven, Conn.: Yale University Press, 1992.

Firestone, Shulamith. *The Dialectic of Sex: The Case for Feminist Revolution.* London: Paladin, 1972.

Gilbert, Neil. "What Do Women Really Want?" *Public Interest,* Winter 2005.

Gordon, Linda. *Woman's Body, Woman's Right: Birth Control in America.* New York: Penguin, 1990.

Greer, Germaine. *The Female Eunuch.* 1970. Reprint, New York: Farrar, Straus & Giroux, 2001.

Hite, Shere. *The Hite Report: A Nationwide Study of Female Sexuality.* 1976. Reprint, New York: Seven Stories Press, 2004.

Kamen, Paula. *Her Way: Young Women Remake the Sexual Revolution.* New York: Broadway Books, 2002.

Kerner, Ian. *She Comes First: The Thinking Man's Guide to Pleasuring a Woman.* New York: Regan Books, 2004.

Lancaster, Roger N. *The Trouble with Nature: Sex in Science and Popular Culture.* Berkeley: University of California Press, 2003.

Laqueur, Thomas. *Making Sex: Body and Gender from the Greeks to Freud.* Cambridge, Mass.: Harvard University Press, 1990.

Lessing, Doris. *The Golden Notebook.* New York: Simon & Schuster, 1962.

Lloyd, Elisabeth A. *The Case of the Female Orgasm: Bias in the Science of Evolution.* Cambridge, Mass.: Harvard University Press, 2005.

Maines, Rachel P. *The Technology of the Orgasm: "Hysteria," the Vibrator, and Women's Sexual Satisfaction.* Baltimore, Md.: Johns Hopkins University Press, 1999.

Margolis, Jonathan. *O: The Intimate History of the Orgasm.* New York: Grove Press, 2004.

Mead, Margaret. *Male and Female: A Study of the Sexes in a Changing World.* New York: William Morrow, 1967.

Meyer, Michael. "Birth Dearth." *Newsweek International,* September 27, 2005.

Michael, Robert T. et al. *Sex in America: A Definitive Survey.* New York: Warner Books, 1994.

Stone, Lawrence. *The Family, Sex, and Marriage in England 1500–1800.* New York: Harper Colophon Books, 1977.

Wallis, Claudia. "The Case for Staying Home." *Time,* March 22, 2004.

DIRT

Berner, Boel. "The Meaning of Cleaning: Producing Harmony and Hygiene in the Home." In *Cultures of Control*, edited by Miriam R. Levin. Amsterdam: Harwood Academic, 2000.

Carson, Anne. "Dirt and Desire: Essay on the Phenomenology of Female Pollution in Antiquity." In *Men in the Off Hours*. New York: Knopf, 2000.

Cowan, Ruth Schwartz. *More Work for Mother: The Ironies of Household Technology from the Open Hearth to the Microwave*. London: Free Association Books, 1989.

Degler, Carl N. "What Ought to Be and What Was: Women's Sexuality in the Nineteenth Century." *American Historical Review,* 79 (1974): 1467–90.

Didion, Joan. *The White Album*. New York: Farrar, Straus & Giroux, 1979.

Dollimore, Jonathan. "Sexual Disgust." *Oxford Literary Review* 20 (1998): 47–77.

Douglas, Mary. *Purity and Danger: An Analysis of Concepts of Pollution and Taboo*. 1966. Reprint. London: Routledge & Kegan Paul, 1978.

Elias, Norbert. *The History of Manners*. 1939. Reprint, New York: Pantheon Books, 1978.

Fellingham, Christine. "Are You Too Clean?" *O, The Oprah Magazine*. September 2002.

Flanagan, Caitlin. "How Serfdom Saved the Women's Movement." *Atlantic Monthly,* March 2004.

Gilmore, David D. *Misogyny: The Male Malady*. Philadelphia: University of Pennsylvania Press, 2001.

Gray, John. *Men Are from Mars, Women Are from Venus: A Practical Guide for Improving Communication and Getting What You Want in Your Relationship*. New York: HarperCollins, 1992.

Hochschild, Arlie Russell. *The Second Shift*. New York: Avon Books, 1989.

Horsfield, Margaret. *Biting the Dust: The Joys of Housework*. London: Fourth Estate, 1997.

Hoy, Suellen. *Chasing Dirt: The American Pursuit of Cleanliness*. New York: Oxford University Press, 1995.

Jeffreys, Sheila. *The Spinster and Her Enemies: Feminism and Sexuality 1880–1930*. London: Pandora Press, 1985.

Kubie, Lawrence S. "The Fantasy of Dirt." *Psychoanalytic Quarterly* 6 (1937): 388–425.

Lasch, Christopher. *Haven in a Heartless World: The Family Besieged.* New York: Basic Books, 1977.

Lerner, Gerda. *The Creation of Patriarchy.* New York: Oxford University Press, 1986.

Maduro, E. S. [pseud.] "Excuse Me While I Explode: My Mother, Myself, and My Anger." In *The Bitch in the House,* edited by Cathi Hanauer. New York: HarperCollins, 2002.

Martin, Bernice. " 'Mother Wouldn't Like It!': Housework as Magic." *Theory, Culture & Society* 2, no. 2 (1984).

Matthews, Glenna. *"Just a Housewife": The Rise and Fall of Domesticity in America.* New York: Oxford University Press, 1987.

Miller, William Ian. *The Anatomy of Disgust.* Cambridge, Mass.: Harvard University Press, 1997.

Moi, Toril. *Simone de Beauvoir: The Making of an Intellectual Woman.* Cambridge, Mass.: Blackwell, 1994.

Olatunji, Bunmi O. "Disgust Sensitivity as a Mediator of the Sex Differences in Contamination Fears." *Personality and Individual Differences* 38 (2005).

Orenstein, Peggy. *Flux: Women on Sex, Work, Love, Kids, and Life in a Half-Changed World.* New York: Anchor, 2000.

Pearson, Allison. *I Don't Know How She Does It.* New York: Anchor Books, 2002.

Rafkin, Louise. *Other People's Dirt: A Housecleaner's Curious Adventures.* New York: Plume, 1999.

Roberts, Tomi-Ann. "Female Trouble: The Menstrual Self-Evaluation Scale and Women's Self-Objectification." *Psychology of Women Quarterly* 28 (2004): 22–26.

———. " 'Feminine Protection': The Effects of Menstruation on Attitudes Toward Women." *Psychology of Women Quarterly* 26 (2002): 131–39.

Rover, Constance. *Love, Morals and the Feminists.* London: Routledge & Kegan Paul, 1970.

Rozin, Paul. "The Borders of the Self: Contamination Sensitivity and Potency of the Body Apertures and Other Body Parts." *Journal of Research in Personality* 29 (1995): 318–40.

Scott, Anne L. "Physical Purity Feminism and State Medicine in Late Nineteenth-Century England." *Women's History Review* 8, no. 4 (1999): 625–53.

Strasser, Susan. *Never Done: A History of American Housework.* New York: Pantheon Books, 1982.

VULNERABILITY

Appignanesi, Lisa, and John Forrester. *Freud's Women.* New York: Basic Books, 1992.

Brownmiller, Susan. *Against Our Will: Men, Women, and Rape.* New York: Simon & Schuster, 1975.

Cahill, Ann J. *Rethinking Rape.* Ithaca, N.Y.: Cornell University Press, 2001.

Coontz, Stephanie. *Marriage, a History: From Obedience to Intimacy or How Love Conquered Marriage.* New York: Viking, 2005.

Deutsch, Helene. "The Significance of Masochism in the Mental Life of Women." 1930; reprinted in *The Psychoanalytic Reader,* edited by Robert Fliess. New York: International Universities Press, Inc., 1948.

Dworkin, Andrea. "The Day I Was Drugged and Raped." *New Statesman,* June 5, 2000.

———. *Intercourse.* New York: Free Press, 1987.

———. *Scapegoat: The Jews, Israel, and Women's Liberation.* New York: Free Press, 2000.

———. "They Took My Body from Me and Used It." *The Guardian,* June 2, 2000.

Ferraro, Kenneth F. "Women's Fear of Victimization: Shadow of Sexual Assault?" *Social Forces* 75, no. 2 (1996): 667–91.

Fliegel, Zenia Odes. "Feminine Psychosexual Development in Freudian Theory: A Historical Reconstruction." *Psychoanalytic Quarterly* 42 (1973): 385–408.

Human Rights Watch. "No Escape: Male Rape in U.S. Prisons." http://www.hrw.org/reports/2001/prison/report.html.

Landers, Elizabeth, and Vicky Mainzer. *The Script: The 100% Absolutely Predictable Things Men Do When They Cheat.* New York: Hyperion, 2005.

MacKinnon, Catharine. *Only Words*. Cambridge, Mass.: Harvard University Press, 1993.

———. *Women's Lives, Men's Laws*. Cambridge, Mass.: Belknap Press, 2005.

Paglia, Camille. *Sexual Personae: Art and Decadence from Nefertiti to Emily Dickinson*. New York: Vintage Books, 1991.

Rainey, Amy. "Sexual Harassment Pervades College Campuses and Injures Men as Well as Women, Survey Finds." *Chronicle of Higher Education*, January 25, 2006.

Rose, Jacqueline. *The Haunting of Sylvia Plath*. Cambridge, Mass.: Harvard University Press, 1992.

Thompson, N. L. "Helene Deutsch: A Life in Theory." *Psychoanalytic Quarterly* 56, no. 2 (1987): 317–53.

U.S. Department of Justice. "Crime in the United States, 2004." (FBI Uniform Crime Report.) http://www.fbi.gov/ucr/cius_04/.

———. "Criminal Victimization, 2004." September 2005. (National Crime Victimization Survey.) http://www.ojp.usdoj.gov/bjs/pub/pdf/cv04.pdf.

———. "Sexual Violence Reported by Correctional Authorities." July 2005. http://www.ojp.usdoj.gov/bjs/pub/pdf/svrc204.pdf.

Warr, Mark. "Fear of Rape Among Urban Women." *Social Problems* 32, no. 3 (1985): 238–50.

———. "Fear of Victimization: Why Are Women and the Elderly More Afraid?" *Social Science Quarterly* 65, no. 3 (1984): 681–702.

Weisberg, Robert, and David Mills. "Violence Silence: Why No One Really Cares About Prison Rape." *Slate*, October 1, 2003.

Wolf, Naomi. *Promiscuities: The Secret Struggle for Womanhood*. New York: Random House, 1997.

———. "Sex and Silence at Yale." *New York*, March 1, 2004.

A NOTE ABOUT THE AUTHOR

Laura Kipnis, a professor of media studies at Northwestern University, has received fellowships from the Guggenheim and Rockefeller foundations and the National Endowment for the Arts. She is the author of *Bound and Gagged: Pornography and the Politics of Fantasy in America; Ecstasy Unlimited: On Sex, Capital, Gender, and Aesthetics;* and *Against Love: A Polemic.* She lives in Chicago and New York.

❜

A NOTE ON THE TYPE

This book was set in Monotype Dante, a typeface designed by Giovanni Mardersteig (1892–1977). Conceived as a private type for the Officina Bodoni in Verona, Italy, Dante was originally cut only for hand composition by Charles Malin, the famous Parisian punch cutter, between 1946 and 1952. Its first use was in an edition of Boccaccio's *Trattatello in laude di Dante* that appeared in 1954. The Monotype Corporation's version of Dante followed in 1957. Although modeled on the Aldine type used for Pietro Cardinal Bembo's treatise *De Aetna* in 1495, Dante is a thoroughly modern interpretation of the venerable face.

Composed by Creative Graphics,
Allentown, Pennsylvania

Printed and bound by R. R. Donnelley & Sons,
Harrisonburg, Virginia

Designed by M. Kristen Bearse